W9-CCO-840

STREETBALL IS LIFE

STREETBALL IS LIFE

Lessons Earned on the Asphalt

Paul Volponi

ROWMAN & LITTLEFIELD
Lanham • Boulder • New York • London

Published by Rowman & Littlefield
An imprint of The Rowman & Littlefield Publishing Group, Inc.
4501 Forbes Boulevard, Suite 200, Lanham, Maryland 20706
www.rowman.com

6 Tinworth Street, London SE11 5AL, United Kingdom

British Library Cataloguing in Publication Information Available

Library of Congress Cataloging-in-Publication Data

Name: Volponi, Paul, author.
Title: Streetball is life : lessons earned on the asphalt / Paul Volponi.
Description: Lanham : Rowman & Littlefield, 2020. | Includes bibliograph-
    ical references. | Summary: "This book is an autobiographical account
    of the author's experiences as a 17-year-old intent on becoming a legiti-
    mate NYC streetballer at the highest level. Included as part of the
    narrative are the important social skills learned on the basketball court,
    showing readers that their time spent streetballing is meaningful be-
    yond the sport itself"—Provided by publisher.
Identifiers: LCCN 2019057221 (print) | LCCN 2019057222 (ebook) |
    ISBN 9781538139271 (cloth) | ISBN 9781538139288 (epub)
Subjects: LCSH: Streetball—New York (State)—New York.
Classification: LCC GV887.3 .V65 2020 (print) | LCC GV887.3 (ebook) |
    DDC 796.323097471—dc23
LC record available at https://lccn.loc.gov/2019057221
LC ebook record available at https://lccn.loc.gov/2019057222

♾ ™ The paper used in this publication meets the minimum requirements
of American National Standard for Information Sciences Permanence of
Paper for Printed Library Materials, ANSI/NISO Z39.48-1992.

"The game of basketball has been everything to me. My place of refuge, place I've always gone where I needed comfort and peace. It's been the site of intense pain and the most intense feelings of joy and satisfaction. It's a relationship that has evolved over time, giving me the greatest respect and love for the game."

—Michael Jordan, six-time NBA champion

CONTENTS

PREFACE

Street basketball is a society of its own. Don't be fooled by the game's often loose and unorganized appearance. It doesn't matter that the participants are usually un-uniformed or even playing "shirts versus skins." I urge you to look closer with a more discerning eye. If you do, you'll discover that the game's inner workings and social rules are highly structured. Because streetball is mostly played without referees or authority figures, the players themselves govern the on-court action, as well as what happens on the sidelines. They control what goes on inside the painted lines of the asphalt court and the chain-link fence surrounding a ball yard. They establish their local constitution, or "park rules," in various ways—sometimes through democratic consensus and other times through the singular force of will of a dominant player.

To thrive and survive in a streetball yard, you need to develop and sharpen a wide array of skills. Many of those skills have nothing to do with ball handling, rebounding, and shooting. Instead, they are advanced social skills. Your ability to communicate, negotiate, problem solve, and deescalate potential conflicts are top among them. Most ballers can confidently look back at their time on a court and point to something in their current lives—a job, a relationship, an achievement—that they've gained through the skills honed while playing streetball. I proudly include myself among them.

Of course, *my* story is really *our* story. That's because streetballers enjoy what is very much a shared experience. It also means that the greatest ballers to ever walk onto the blacktop—legends with tags such as Dr. J, Black Mamba, Helicopter, Hawk, The Goat, Destroyer, Hot Sauce, Bone Collector, The Professor, and Big Dipper—have all to some extent traveled paths similar to the rest of us.

At this collective story's conclusion, you'll learn about the lives of some of these legends, as well as some of the famed ball yards, films, literature, fashion, commerce, and language spawned by streetball culture. And, of course, you'll learn how streetball enhances the skills needed to succeed in life.

So the next time someone scowls at you and asks, "Are you going to waste your time playing ball again today?" your uplifting reply can be, "Waste my time? No. I'm about to participate in and become part of a complex society of ever-shifting tribes [teams] while I sharpen a wide array of skills to enhance my future."

PROLOGUE

I fell in love with basketball at sixteen. Not with watching it on TV or wearing a numbered jersey with my name arching across the back. I'm talking about the actual game. Becoming part of the rhythm and flow of ten players searching for their place in something that lives and breathes. Something that strives to move with one mind. One goal. One passion. To be a member of the winning squad and stay on the court, sending the losers to the end of a long line of fresh opponents waiting for the next game.

Other than those players waiting to get onto the court, there were no crowds. No spectators beyond occasional passersby who'd put down their grocery bags for a moment to stare at the intense conflict on the other side of a chain-link fence. The lack of cheers and adulation didn't matter, though. Those were never the motivation. Streetball is strictly fueled by pride and desire. And those undocumented battles were mostly contested with the same ferocity as the NBA finals.

When the game seduced me, LeBron James hadn't been born yet, Kobe Bryant was still in diapers, and nobody wanted to "be like Mike" because Michael Jordan was about to be cut from his high school's varsity basketball team and sent to the JV squad.

There was never a realistic thought of becoming a pro or even being offered a college scholarship. The rock rarely bounces that

"I wanted somebody pushing me. I wanted to have you try to take my heart. I wanted to test my chest against your chest. . . . If you don't know what it is to leave a basketball court crying. If you don't know what it is to leave a basketball court bleeding. Then you don't really understand basketball." — Richard "Pee Wee" Kirkland, streetball icon

way for streetballers. Instead, we play out of an overwhelming need to express ourselves and to compete against anyone with the guts to enter the park. Those who don't understand us see this passion as a dead end, a waste of time and energy without a tangible payoff. Our critics mistakenly value the perceived destination over the enlightening journey.

Streetballers are always searching for their Nirvana—a streetball paradise where the competition and commitment to the game reflects their own. I found mine at a place called the Proving Ground during the summer I graduated high school.

The Proving Ground was a ball yard where teens knocked heads against grown men—mostly cops, firemen, and construction and sanitation workers who gladly leveraged their considerable strength and weight against yours. There were no simple fouls in this particular version of streetball, just hits delivered so hard that they resembled felonies.

If you made a sweet jumper inside the gates of the Proving Ground, you didn't dare smile or celebrate too loudly. If you did, someone was coming to knock you down. But if you canned a second shot in a row, you might as well celebrate. Because opposing players were going to physically punish you anyway. The park's culture resembled that of the Roman Colosseum as much as it did Madison Square Garden. And despite the bone-jarring nature of its overly competitive contests, the basketball played there was nothing but pure.

The Proving Ground was a difficult place to cultivate friendships and an easy place to make enemies, at least until new sides were chosen at the end of every game. But if you could earn the respect of the players there, you could hold your head up high and walk with confidence anywhere.

This is the story of my summer-long initiation at the Proving Ground. It is truly a streetball crucible of a teen who wanted more than anything else in the world to earn his stripes, staking his claim as a legitimate streetballer. I didn't understand at the time that this experience would deliver to me a set of skills that enhanced my life far beyond the boundaries of a basketball court.

I

LEAVING THE COMFORT ZONE

You begin by playing against your friends. They're kids from your immediate neighborhood. Kids who truly believe they have a love for the game. Over time, however, you realize that you're different. Your team almost always wins. And when it comes time to choose up sides, you're usually picked first.

Soon you find yourself alone on a court, shooting baskets long after the sun goes down. You're playing on the one bent rim in the park because it's the only hoop illuminated by a streetlight. Or maybe you've talked a relative into bringing their car up to the fence and turning on the headlights. You're hungry for a game. But your friends are all off doing something else. That's when you realize you're ready for the next step. You need to leave the comfort zone of your neighborhood yard and test yourself against better players.

For me, that came about during the spring of my senior year in high school. It meant leaving the hoops nestled beneath the Triborough Bridge (now renamed the Robert F. Kennedy Bridge) in Queens, New York. They were courts shielded from the harsh elements of the world by the immense six-lane roadway approximately sixty feet overhead.

Still uncertain of myself, I took a lateral sidestep, four blocks west to a second section of courts under the bridge. Those courts drew players from other neighborhoods and housing developments.

The rising roadway was probably 150 feet overhead there, high enough to allow in the slashing winds and rain.

I didn't have any siblings or a best friend to use as a sounding board, to give me feedback about my plans. There wasn't a girl I'd dated more than two or three times. Most streetballers are loners. It comes with the territory, the solo hours of practice invested in polishing your game.

My parents both worked, living paycheck to paycheck, while never owning a house or a car. They really hadn't succeeded at anything in life, except being great people. Their biggest claim to fame had been raising me, a B– student who never mouthed off to his teachers. Only I desperately wanted something more. And I found it in the feeling of a basketball balanced on my fingertips.

"You're just like your old man," Dad told me. "I played basketball in the street all the time. I was crazy for the game."

I'd nod my head in response and smile, just to make him feel good. But deep down, I knew his love affair with the game hadn't burned anywhere as fiery as mine. I could tell by the coolness in his stories and the way he held the ball in his hands instead of cradling it.

As a streetballer, I could pass and shoot the rock with some touch. More importantly, I played defense with an immense chip on my shoulder, taking every point scored against me as a personal insult.

My skills stood up to the new surroundings, and I quickly bonded with four other players: Angelo, Monk, Hot Rod Rodriguez, and Jumbo. It was easy to see that we shared the same intense passion to play. Together, we became a makeshift team ready to travel to any yard in the five boroughs to stamp ourselves as recognized New York City streetballers.

Like me, Angelo and Monk were high school seniors. Angelo was the sharpest jump shooter I'd ever seen, although he didn't look anything like a basketball player. He was six-foot even, with a frame that was round and soft. He was the real-life Woody Harrelson character (Billy Hoyle) from *White Men Can't Jump* a decade before that movie was made. Angelo had learned to shoot the rock by practicing night and day in his backyard, fine-tuning a high-arching jumper over his mother's clothesline. His house was a half mile from the courts. After every game, he'd phone home to make sure his mom had a meal ready for him. His conversation with her, mostly in Greek, would be punctuated by a handful of words I understood.

"Ma . . . pork chops . . . french fries," he'd emphasize, interrupting the flow of her native tongue.

Monk was a stone-cold preppy. He only wore the newest kicks and changed the laces every week to keep them spotless. His shirt was always tucked into his shorts, even if he had to stop playing mid-game to fix it. He was tall and lanky. For a nice guy, Monk was amazingly annoying, often pointing out everyone else's faults. And though other players were jealous of Monk's ideal basketball body, they mostly viewed him as someone who'd never worked hard enough to get the most out of it.

Hot Rod Rodriguez was a few years older. He'd done a hitch in the army and had a job on the nightshift as a doorman at a swanky Manhattan apartment building. He stood five feet, nine inches tall and was built like a short-armed fire hydrant. Hot Rod couldn't shoot, dribble, or pass. What he could do, though, was station himself directly in front of you and play defense. He'd somehow injured his right wrist in the military and couldn't make a normal layup without turning it into an odd-angled adventure.

I started calling Hot Rod "Fifty-Fifty" because those were the realistic odds of him sinking a breakaway layup.

Jumbo gave our quintet size, a presence beneath the boards and in the paint. He was six foot two and a good thirty-five to forty pounds overweight. That didn't stop him from being amazingly agile and moving like a chunky ballerina with octopus arms. Jumbo had a full-time job reading electric meters for Con Edison. Every day, he'd read the minimum number of meters on his route before marking everyone else N/A (not available). Then Jumbo would ditch his blue Con Edison work shirt and meet us at the courts. Equally as important, Jumbo had a car—a brown two-door economy model. It was a four-seater into which the five of us jammed to

"All your life you are told the things you cannot do. All your life they will say you're not good enough or strong enough or talented enough. They will say you're the wrong height or the wrong weight or the wrong type to play this or be this or achieve this. They will tell you no. A thousand times no. Until all the no's become meaningless. All your life they will tell you no. Quite firmly and very quickly. And you will tell them yes." —LeBron James, Akron, Ohio, native and three-time NBA champion, who as a youngster fought to over-come his harsh inner-city environment barnstorm the city's b-ball yards. Jumbo named her "Brown Betty" after his favorite dessert of apples baked with brown sugar. Being our thinnest member, I routinely rode the hump in the middle of her backseat.

"Unless somebody goes on a diet or I decide to leave Monk stranded in some park, that's your official spot, your half-seat," Jumbo needled me.

My streetball game was in its infancy. At six feet tall and 165 pounds, I shied away from physical contact, using my speed to find open jumpers. My pops was left-handed, so I'd emulated him. As a natural righty, I'd become almost ambidextrous and could shoot the ball with both hands.

Not long after our team's birth, I earned a nickname. While I was playing shirtless on a sunny June day, somebody's unleashed Rottweiler grabbed my T-shirt in its saliva-soaked mouth and refused to give it back. That's when Angelo gave me the tag "Pets." Whenever we went into the store across the street from the courts for chips and drinks, the rest of the guys would point at the sign in the window that read "No Pets Allowed."

We were hardly an intimidating-looking crew. But as a streetball squad, we knew each other's moves—strengths and weaknesses—allowing us to play well over our athletic ceilings. We came away with surprising victories in hugely competitive yards such as Central Park and Dyckman Park.

At Manhattan Beach (located in Brooklyn), we held the court for almost two hours, winning several games in a row. The locals were completely pissed and put together a team of goons to physically beat us into the asphalt. Jumbo exchanged a series of vicious elbows with their biggest threat, who became even angrier at his daring to fight back.

"If you can't take it, don't dish it out!" Jumbo barked.

That's when the guy tightly gripped the rock between his huge paws. From maybe ten feet away, he fired it overhand at Jumbo, who caught it cleanly in his hands as if he were king of the dodgeball court. In response, Jumbo punted the ball over the fence and onto the sandy beach, where it bounced toward the ocean.

A wild fight broke out between us and what seemed like every player we'd defeated that afternoon. I ducked a few phantom punches and heard Monk's voice from behind me shouting, "Cooler heads, guys! Cooler heads!"

That melee probably lasted for less than a minute, before three times our number chased us out of the park and across the boulevard to where Brown Betty was parked. We jumped inside in record time and then sped away with a small mob chasing us down the street.

No one was hurt. All the way home, we laughed and bragged about our performance the way a tight-knit army platoon might after surviving an ambush. It was a great streetball experience. Something that would ultimately serve us well. Though we had no idea at the time, over the course of the next few Saturdays, we'd take the first steps down a brutal gauntlet. One that would offer us the opportunity to raise our streetball reputation to another level.

2

INTO THE FIRE

The principal called my name, and I walked across the stage to receive my high school diploma. After the ceremony, in the back of the auditorium, my grandma asked if I had any plans for the summer.

I knew better than to tell her that I was focused on playing ball. She'd already twice mentioned that a similar-aged cousin of mine was going to Europe for a few weeks. But the only traveling I had a passion for was to visit as many streetball yards as possible over the next two months.

"My uncle on my mom's side owns a gas station," I answered her, just to fill space. "I've been getting a few hours of work there, on and off."

Dad gave me a long sideways glance. He knew they'd stripped my hours at the station down to nothing because I'd sent three cars on their way without reattaching their gas caps one Saturday afternoon. My uncle claimed it was because I had my mind on something else—being at the b-ball courts.

"I just want him to stay out of trouble before he starts college in September," added Dad. "That simple."

"Our son doesn't get into trouble," Mom defended me. "Just into fights at basketball."

I'd actually never thrown a punch at anyone who hadn't started with me first. On the flip side of that—lots of players took offense at how hard I competed against them. They took my style of harassing defense personally and probably felt justified in picking their hands up to me.

Mom had me pegged right though.

I was the kind of kid you wanted to find your lost wallet on the street. I'd read your ID, get your address, and bring that wallet straight back with the money still inside. But if I ever met you on the court, I'd be hell-bent to pick your pocket of the basketball and steal your pride.

*   *   *

On the Saturday before the Fourth of July, it was ninety-seven degrees with a sky-rocketing humidity. Just being outside was like standing in the shower, with salty beads of sweat stinging at my eyes.

The five of us piled into Jumbo's car and drove off in search of run. There was no air-conditioning in the Brown Betty. Monk hung his head out the back window in the breeze, like a well-groomed dog. We drove from yard to yard around the city, looking for a game. But every deep well of basketball had seemingly dried up for the day in the intense heat. We only encountered small kids, inferior players, or dudes who didn't want to step out of the cool shade to compete.

"We understand. You don't want to get your butts whipped," Hot Rod told some guys in one yard.

Even that slap-in-the-face challenge didn't deliver us a game.

After chipping in for gas, Angelo, Monk, and I had less than two bucks in our combined pockets. We pooled our money together, and Angelo decided he'd be the one to go into the nearest deli alone.

He came out carrying a two-liter bottle of root beer.

"That bottle's not sweating," I said. "Is it warm?"

"I don't like it too cold. It bothers my teeth," answered Angelo, who demanded to drink his entire share first before passing the bottle to anyone else.

"You can finish it," I told Monk. "I don't want any warm back-wash."

By 11:30 a.m., Jumbo had had enough of driving. He was ready to drop us off beneath the Triborough Bridge. I was a firm holdout, though, still looking to satisfy my basketball jones.

"I know one last place. Maybe fifteen blocks north of here. It's a yard next to the Triborough Bus Company's big garage," I said. "My dad used to take me there when I was a kid. I think it's got three full courts laid out side by side."

Dad had taken me there for my eighth birthday to shoot hoops. We'd played together for a while before five guys on the next court cajoled him into joining them for three-on-three. That left me alone with a ball in my hands, fighting back the tears. Now I couldn't blame him for wanting to compete. But back then, I didn't under-stand it.

"I've played there in the past," said Hot Rod. "It's got kiddie sprinklers too."

"Okay, that sold me," said Jumbo, with the steering wheel turn-ing north like a compass needle. "But if there's no game, I'm going under those sprinklers to cool off. Doesn't matter if it's filled with five-year-olds. I'm going in."

As we pulled up to the place, the Department of Parks sign on the fence read "Woodtree Playground." Beneath that, scratched into the sign, was a grouping of uneven letters that spelled out "Proving Ground."

Slipping through a huge hole in the chain-link fence, we saw close to twenty players at the far end of the yard, gathered around wooden benches and several ice coolers. At that moment, in the desert-like heat, the yard seemed to hover somewhere between a mirage and a streetball oasis. Angelo immediately began to bounce the ball in his hand to announce our arrival.

Most of those players, a mixture of teens and adults, picked their heads up to see. But not a single one of them acknowledged our presence. They just stayed glued to those benches, glistening with sweat, coldly ignoring us and looking tough as nails.

We began to warm up—stretching, jumping, passing around the rock, and knocking down jumpers. Still, there was nothing from those guys.

Finally, Hot Rod approached them. Only he completely abandoned that challenging tone he'd used earlier in the day. And there wasn't a doubt in my mind that these dudes would have pounded us if he hadn't.

"You guys interested in going full court? We've got our five," he said. "You want to put out a team?"

Their eyes seemed to turn toward a few of their key players. Without a verbal response, one of them stood up from the bench and demonstratively shook his head before leaving the yard.

We'd already endured a three-hour odyssey around the scorched city in search of run. A shake of somebody's head wasn't about to stop us. We kept shooting the ball on that court, laying down our best moves and hoping to entice a game.

Over the next fifteen minutes, that crowd of players slowly shrank in number until only one remained. He was probably in his mid-thirties, standing five foot ten and weighing approximately 260 pounds of chiseled muscle. His softer face was framed by a curly black beard. He planted his toes at the edge of the court, watching us with a bottle of beer in his hand. In my mind, I imagined him suddenly lowering his head like a rhino and charging through the concrete handball walls there for fun.

"You want to play three-on-three," Jumbo asked him.

"Nah, my muscles are stiff already from sitting. I don't want to strain anything," he replied. "We've been playing all morning."

The rock bounced off the rim directly to him. He put his beer down on the hot asphalt and picked the ball up over his head with two hands. Then he shotput it toward the basket, missing the iron hoop and nearly breaking the backboard.

The five of us might have been thinking it, but no one had the courage to shout, "Brick!"

"We're here every Saturday," he said. "If you guys are looking for a game, show up next week at nine o'clock sharp. But I'll warn you, it's going to be rough. We don't give strangers a free pass. It's just the opposite. You need to prove you can stand up here. Anyway, I'm Reggie."

By the time we finished introducing ourselves, Big Reggie was already headed for the gate, carrying a huge cooler in his arms. He put it into the trunk of a yellow Cadillac convertible. Then he climbed into the driver's seat and started up the engine.

Before he drove off, Reggie hollered, "Don't hurt yourselves. Save that for next week."

We all stopped playing and just looked at each other. There was no way we weren't going to be back here the following Saturday. Only we knew better than to walk in at 9 a.m. and be behind their regulars, stuck on the sidelines. So we made a pact to be standing on that same court by 8:15 and to have our five ready to rock and roll.

For almost another half hour, we shot the ball on both rims, trying to get the feel of that full court. When we'd finished, every one of us hit the sprinklers. And Jumbo, true to his word, waded way out into the middle of the shallow pool like a baby elephant, splashing and making waves for all the little kids there.

SELF-REFLECTION: INTERDEPENDENCE

There's a concept in sociology (the study of human society) termed "interdependence." And it's so important you can't have a society without it. Interdependence refers to when two or more people are dependent on each other to achieve the things they desire. It's easy to see how teammates are interdependent, working for the same goals. But it goes well beyond that. In streetball, you can't test yourself without finding a willing and suitable opponent, someone whose commitment to the game mirrors your own. That's why my teammates and I wanted to play against the very best competition. In turn, our opponents were equally dependent on us to achieve their goals. That actually made our opposing groups interdependent, creating the basis of a larger streetball society. To the casual observer it probably looked like nothing more than two teams competing on the court. But we were actually opening the door to participating in a complex social structure, the blending of two distinctly different tribes in an effort to satisfy the needs of each. Hence, streetballers embrace the idea of competition, a vital quality needed to advance in life.

3

STAKING OUR CLAIM

The stifling weather refused to break. By the following Friday night, the walls of our small apartment had absorbed every bit of that intense heat. We even had cold cuts for dinner because Mom passed on the idea of adding to that inferno by turning on the kitchen stove.

The only air-conditioning in the house was in my parents' bedroom. Unfortunately, I was too old to sleep in there with them. The stagnant airflow inside my narrow room made it nearly impossible to breathe, even with the window opened wide. So I slept on the living room floor, where it was a few degrees cooler, my sweat seeping into the thin carpeting.

I tossed and turned most of the night—partly from the heat and partly from my muscles twitching to the moves I dreamed about laying down on that court the next morning.

We were the first five players to show up at the Proving Ground. Despite the early hour, the mercury had already climbed past the ninety-degree mark.

"Don't warm up too hard," cautioned Hot Rod. "Reserve some energy. We're going to need it."

We were occupying the same court as the week before. Of the three full courts in a row, it was the one closest to the benches, water fountains, and street parking. We weren't about to budge for any reason. If those guys were going to try to play without including us, they'd have to move their game.

One by one their players began to arrive, gathering at the basket opposite the one we held. None of them had spoken a word to us yet. Among them was a teen who couldn't have been any taller than five foot five, his arms covered in snake tattoos. I swear he hissed at us before spitting just off the court.

Next, a dude bordering on three hundred pounds walked in. He was definitely a few years older than me, and his mouth turned out to be as big as his belly.

"These guys got some nerve," he complained from behind a thick black moustache. "I can't believe they're back, standing on that court like they own it. This is *our* park! We may have to give them more than an education!"

That was music to my competitive ears, because that Round Mound of Attitude sounded like has was actually willing to play us.

The instant their fifth player arrived, Jumbo smartly walked over and arranged the game, before any extra bodies might argue to take our place.

"Park rules. We choose up sides among the first ten to show up," said Snake, pounding his dribble on the asphalt. "But screw that. We'll play our guys against yours. Game's sixteen by ones. Eight half. That's when we switch baskets."

It had been seven days of anxious anticipation for me. Now the moment of truth was finally here.

"Give us a minute or two to warm up," sneered Round Mound. "You guys were probably here since 6 a.m. getting loose, trying to sandbag us in this heat."

Angelo understood that those other five were now checking us out, to see whom they should guard. That's when Angelo began missing shots badly, throwing up total bricks, hoping he'd draw their worst defender.

My eyes had settled on their fifth player to enter the park. He'd pulled up in a beat-up car with a big wooden ladder strapped to the roof. He had to be in his forties and was whisper thin, like a whip.

Jumbo said, "That's the window washer from Steinway Street, where all the big stores are. I've seen him work. He carries that heavy ladder around like a feather."

His teammates were calling him "Pirate," almost genuflecting in his presence. He ran a hand back through his uncombed red hair before he popped some dental work out of his mouth and stuffed it into his pocket. Then he drained a smooth jumper from the corner and proclaimed, "I'm ready. Let's get this thing started. Our ball first."

Pirate walked across the court toward us and flashed a jack-o-lantern grin, with an open space of five or six teeth missing across the top front.

Suddenly, I remembered him. It had to be six or seven years ago. I was at the courts in my neighborhood, beneath the Triborough Bridge. There were just three of us in the yard—two guys in their late teens playing one-on-one against each other, and me. I'd asked a bunch of times for them to let me into the game, but I was being ignored. That's when Pirate walked in, not that I'd ever asked his name. He marched up to those guys and demanded to play.

"I'll take the kid on my side," he'd told them, pointing to me and displaying that near-toothless smile. "And it's still not going to be a game you can win."

Pirate only let me touch the ball to check it out of bounds. He took every shot and scored every basket on his own, with me standing around as decoration. At one point, both guys were guarding Pirate, understanding that he wouldn't pass me the rock. That's when he laid down the greatest move I'd ever seen. He blew past the first dude and then put the second on his hip. In one lightning-quick motion, Pirate hid the ball behind his back while simultaneously slapping the defender on his backside, making him believe the ball had been passed away. The guy frantically turned around to find me. Only Pirate still had the rock and swished it into the hoop.

"I don't even think that's legal," complained the defender. "You can't touch me like that."

One play later, Pirate purposely elbowed him in the ribs so hard that the dude lost his breath and could barely finish.

"First off, it's a time investment [to develop skills]. Nobody gets good at something in a week. . . . To master something you really need to put in mass hours. So having a passion goes a long way. . . . People try to place streetball in like a genre. But I think that's only because a couple of [famous] players back in the day were doing illegal moves. . . . For the most part, it was just basketball in the summer, which is obviously looser, where guys can utilize flash more. But to me it's all basketball." —Grayson "The Professor" Boucher, an Oregon native and ball-handling sensation with the AND1 Mixtape Tour and Ball Up Tour

I think we won that game by a score of 15–2.

"That'll teach those bums a lesson," Pirate had told me before he left the park. "And it could have been worse for them."

Standing on the court alone, I couldn't decide if Pirate was some kind of streetball superhero or if he belonged locked up behind bars.

Now, as Pirate and his four teammates started up the court at us, Hot Rod pointed at Pirate and said to me, "Pets, you guard the old man. Watch him close. I've seen him play before. He's tricky and dirty."

I swallowed hard and stepped to my defensive assignment.

Meanwhile, Big Reggie had entered the yard. He'd taken a seat on his cooler, just inches from the court.

Slapping his huge hands together like a thunderclap, Reggie said, "Damn, I slept too late. I knew they'd be here early. I wish I was out there. But at least I'm in the front row. This is going to be better than cable TV."

4

THE BATTLE WITHIN

The first time Pirate had the ball in his hands, he darted for the baseline. For somebody in his forties, he was incredibly quick. I'd run track for a few years in high school. But Pirate moved sideways almost as fast as I could go forward.

I hustled my behind to the baseline to cut him off. As soon as I committed my speed in that direction, Pirate stopped on a dime. Then he faded away and released a feathery jumper that just ticked the rim going in.

We weren't behind on the score long. Snake was guarding Angelo and not taking him the least bit seriously. He was giving Angelo four feet of room from straight on at the top of the key. Angelo buried the first shot with a *thump* as the ball ricocheted down off the iron.

"He'll never do that again," said Snake, as Angelo kept his facial expression totally blank. "I'll let you shoot from there all day."

On our next possession, we worked the rock right back to Angelo at the same spot. The result was identical, another nailed jumper.

"Guard him!" Pirate snapped at Snake.

"That boy doesn't look like a ballplayer. But he can shoot!" shouted Reggie from the sideline.

I cut Pirate off from receiving the ball, and the Round Mound turned it over. Jumbo picked it up and found Monk streaking ahead of the field. His layup put us on top 3–1.

I was chasing Pirate from behind. But before he could get his hands on the ball, Snake, trying to get even with Angelo, hoisted up a long jumper. The instant the ball left his fingertips, Angelo took off in the opposite direction.

Jumbo grabbed the rebound and quickly shuttled me the rock. I hit Monk with a frozen rope of a pass. In turn, Monk delivered the ball to Angelo, who was far ahead of the field, for an easy basket.

"He's just basket-hanging!" raged Round Mound. "Anybody can do that if they don't want to play D!"

Our lead stood at 4–1.

Pirate was cursing all the way up the court, nearly foaming at the mouth in anger. He demanded the ball from his teammates and got it. Then he dribbled straight at me. Pirate turned and shoved his hip into mine. It was the very beginning of that incredible move I'd seen him make years ago. Only I was more than ready, because I'd pictured that move in my mind maybe a thousand times since. He hid the ball behind his back and in the same motion slapped at my backside. Pirate even made the sound of wind with his mouth—*phhhst*—as if the ball had flown past me. But I didn't turn to chase that noise. Instead, I reached behind him and knocked the rock away.

It was rolling loose on the asphalt. I had all the forward momentum and beat Pirate to the ball. I looked up, and Angelo was running free down the sideline. I looped him the pass and watched as he buried a short banker.

Now the score was 5–1.

I could never have predicted what happened next. Pirate completely lost it and charged in my direction. His eyes were wild, maybe even more fearsome than his grin. Other than Snake, Pirate was the only one on the court who didn't have twenty pounds on me. So once I realized that I couldn't sidestep him, my only option was to put my head down and go right into him.

We collided at center court. That's when I heard a loud *snap*.

I felt for my chest and arms to see if I was still in one piece. But before I could come up with any definite conclusions, I heard Pirate scream in pain.

He was doubled over, with his left arm hanging low. People started pouring onto the court from the sideline to check him out.

"I've seen this before," Hot Rod told Pirate. "I think you've dislocated your collarbone."

That's when Pirate ran toward the fence. With his good arm, he grabbed a broken piece of wood. Then he came at me, swinging it overhead like a club.

"Look out, Pets!" hollered Jumbo, pushing me away.

Big Reggie and another Proving Ground regular named Gene the Dream wrestled Pirate down and took that makeshift club away. Then Gene practically dragged Pirate toward his car to drive him to the hospital.

"I'll get even with you!" Pirate screamed at me, making his forced exit. "I'll get even with your whole damn team! None of you belong here!"

"You did this to yourself, old man," Gene lectured him. "You're not indestructible. I can prove it. That lightweight kid just cracked you."

I was breathing hard, bouncing on my toes as the car pulled away from the curb. Adrenaline was rushing through my veins, and I couldn't come close to standing still.

The break in the basketball game didn't last long.

"I got Pirate's spot," said Reggie, stepping onto the court. "I hate to come on because of an injury. But let's do this thing. I'm ready."

A guy named Surfer Joe, a shirtless, blonde California-type, took Gene the Dream's place.

"I wouldn't want to be in your shoes," Surfer Joe told me. "You're going to have a target on your back."

"We don't play scared. Pets is a baller," Jumbo responded. "Just another day on the court for us."

"Listen to these guys," said Round Mound. "They think they're tough now. Warriors. They haven't lasted here more than ten minutes yet. Not even half a game."

I was trying to look confident. But on the inside, I was shaking, feeling all the wrong kinds of goosebumps and fighting hard to hold it together. I'd been in plenty of scraps with other players. But never one as senseless and violent as that, and especially not with an adult.

When the game restarted, the rock came to me. I was standing wide open, a few feet past the foul line, at the right elbow. That was one of my favorite spots. I took a deep breath and shot the ball. Only it didn't hit a thing—not the rim or the backboard.

"Nice air ball," said Round Mound in a hefty voice dripping with sarcasm. "Nerves of steel."

The rest of that game I kept my head on a swivel, with an eye out for who might try to even up the score with me.

Reggie was recklessly throwing his body around, like someone had taught a grizzly bear how to play basketball. But I could tell it wasn't anything personal. That was just his overly physical style.

I didn't accomplish much the rest of that game, except not to break down and bawl. We won easy, 16–6. I did sink our final basket though, a running one-hander in the lane. As a team, we were stoked by that victory. Only we didn't do much high-fiving because we knew those guys wanted their revenge.

We won the next game too and only lost the third when Hot Rod refused to call a pair of fouls after getting hammered by Big Reggie.

"The only credit I'll give you guys is that you don't whine when you get hit," said the Round Mound.

When that first morning at the Proving Ground had finished, I didn't want any part of the hump in the Brown Betty's backseat. I decided to walk home alone. Just to make the point that I didn't need anyone's protection.

Then I left that yard with my head held high. Only I kept my eyes opened wide for the first few blocks, especially after Snake, who was driving a sleek Corvette Stingray, slowed down to glare at me. But all he did was rev the engine hot and then roar away.

SELF-REFLECTION: GROUP DYNAMICS

Another important element of a society is "likeness." That means members of a group have something in common and in some way are vitally alike. My teammates were all at different stages of life. Angelo, Monk, and I were graduating high school. Hot Rod, an army vet, and Jumbo, who had a wife and kids, were adults with full-time jobs. Normally, our differences would stop us from forming a close friendship. But those differences were overcome by our likeness—our mutual desire to prove ourselves on a streetball court. Most streetballers are exposed to a wide array of people during their time on a court. They become comfortable meeting and interacting with others of different ages and backgrounds—with basketball as the common denominator between them. It is a quality that will undoubtedly serve them well in the future.

5

ONE-ON-ONE WAR

Throughout that next week, I did hundreds of pushups and sit-ups. I was getting ready for what I figured would be my fight with Pirate, or his proxy, that coming Saturday. I started out on Monday morning at Astoria Park, sprinting a fast, flat mile. Then I did several laps around the quarter-mile track there, running backward and slide-stepping sideways in a defensive basketball crouch.

My eyes were focused on the ground in front of me. That's when I saw a second shadow closing in on mine. Before I could spin around, it leaped into the air and came crashing down on my shoulders.

"There he is, the marked man," said Angelo, who'd come jogging up from behind and grabbed me in a bear hug. "*Arrrrr!* Be careful that Pirate doesn't make you walk the plank."

"Think it could get that ugly?" I asked as we began to jog together.

"He only tried to beat you with a wooden club," Angelo replied. "Anything could happen. Those guys are maniacs. You know how many times I took a jumper and one of them tried to get under my feet to make me sprain an ankle. Reggie seems like the only normal one, and he's *naturally* out of control. Monk thinks we should call it quits down there. We already won week one. What's to gain?"

"Not me. I'm going back," I said with total conviction. "If it's pouring rain, thunder and lightning, I'll be standing there next Saturday. Just to prove the point."

Getting into a throw-down with Pirate was the last thing I wanted. I wasn't even sure that I could survive a fight with him. That he wouldn't wipe the yard with me. But there was something I feared much more: losing the respect of everyone at the Proving Ground. Deep down, I knew that getting past this one-on-one war with Pirate would take me a long way in earning a reputation as a streetballer.

On Wednesday night, our five-man squad met at the courts beneath the Triborough Bridge. We played one game against another group of guys. But we just sailed past them without an ounce of real resistance.

"We might be wasting our time here now," said Jumbo, who'd barely broken a sweat. "It's just a good tune-up for Saturday. Nothing more."

Monk was campaigning for us not to go back to the Proving Ground.

"It's not basketball. There are no rules. It's like that movie *Rollerball* come to life. You could win, lose, or die there," said Monk.

"Hey, I've been in the army with live rounds of ammo going over my head. This isn't life and death," said Hot Rod. "The actual basketball part is good. They make the right pass to the open guy and play tough defense."

"Yeah, they stress the fundamentals and violence," quipped Angelo, behind a wry smile.

"I'm starting at an elite university in September," said Monk, who'd been accepted into Lehigh in Pennsylvania. "Do I really need to spend time with these cutthroats and maybe begin the semester with a broken leg?"

Angelo was going to be a freshman at NYU, while I'd gotten into a city college by the skin of my teeth.

College hadn't been in my original plans. But I'd gotten a taste of the working world when UPS hired me to sort packages for the Christmas rush. I stood in front of a loud conveyor belt with six empty trailer trucks behind me. I had to memorize the route of each truck, putting the packages into the right one. I'd grab two boxes at a time. One might be addressed "Albany" and another "Fishkill." I'd tuck each beneath an arm before seeing a third box rolling toward me marked "Troy." Then I'd forget which box was already under what arm, and I'd have to read them both again. That's when the belt would suddenly increase speed. The packages piled up at the end of the conveyor, eventually falling to the floor. The boss would rip me in front of everybody. UPS didn't fire me until after Christmas. But they wrote on my personnel chart in big letters "UN-MOTIVATED." That hurt because I felt like they didn't even know me.

"What do you say, Pets?" asked Monk. "You've probably got the most to lose with the Pirate after you."

"I just want to play ball. I'll deal with the rest, if that's the trade-off," I answered, trying to convince myself as much as anybody else. "But I'm going back there."

Then Jumbo told Monk, "We whipped the players here tonight because our last game was against stronger competition. We already owe those lunatics something, even Pirate."

The soles of my kicks had nearly worn out. I never wanted to break in a new pair on the court and risk getting blisters that might ruin my game. So I always bought new sneakers in advance and would get used to them just walking around.

That Friday, I went up to Steinway Street to shop at the sneaker stores. It was more than a mile walk from my house in the blazing heat. By the time I got there, I was sweating up a storm. Approaching the first sneaker place, I saw Pirate's wooden ladder leaned up against a bank's tall glass window panes, a squeegee and some rags at its base. Pirate's car was parked at the curb beside it. Only Pirate was nowhere in sight.

A chill shot up and down my spine. With my next step, I turned in the opposite direction and started walking away, twice as fast. The only positive thing I could say about myself is that I wasn't running.

I didn't get much sleep that night and even shadow-boxed my bedroom wall a few times.

The next morning, I decided to leave for the Proving Ground early, at around 7:25 a.m. Jumbo had asked me if I wanted a ride. I guess he was concerned about me getting caught there alone. But I'd turned him down.

I took a basketball with me, and before I left the house, I wrote my name on it in capital letters with Mom's indelible laundry marker: "PAUL VOLPONI." Then I dribbled the rock all the way there to get myself in a good rhythm and occupy my mind.

As I walked through the gates of the Proving Ground, my ears were tuned to the sound of two things—the rock pounding the pavement and the loud beating of my heart.

For nearly fifteen minutes, I shot the ball alone on the court. Then beyond the chain-link fence, I heard a car pulling up. It was Pirate's. I held the rock close to my chest and watched him walk into the park with his left arm in a sling.

"Come over here, you prick," he said, in a tone that probably could have sounded a lot more threatening. "Look at what you did. You think this stopped me? I worked my regular route cleaning windows all week with a busted wing."

I wasn't sure what to say. But what came from my mouth was, "I'm sorry you got hurt."

"This is nothing. I've broken lots of bones playing ball," he said before he swiped the rock from my grasp with his good arm.

Pirate dribbled halfway down the court and sank a long one-handed set shot.

Then he walked back to the bench and began to lace up his kicks—a pair of black Chuck Taylor high-tops with a small section of canvas cut out to avoid blisters on his little toe.

"You go to school or something?" Pirate asked.

"I start college in September," I answered.

"So you're good at reading, with books and things," he said. I nodded my head. "There's nothing wrong with that. Keep studying. Don't be in a hurry to work. That's what I tell my daughter, and she's older than you."

"With the more success through basketball, the more confident I became, and the more I learned how to have a greater voice, and learned how to love myself." —Cheryl Miller, Basketball Hall of Famer

"Thanks. I will," I said, breathing much easier.

There was a long pause, as if Pirate was finished with me. So I walked off to retrieve the rock. When I got back to the bench, Jumbo was already parking the Brown Betty. He had Angelo in the front seat, riding shotgun. At about the same time, Gene the Dream, Surfer Joe, and Snake arrived. They were followed by Hot Rod and Big Reggie.

None of the Proving Ground regulars seemed surprised that Pirate was about to play with a dislocated collarbone.

"Hi, Mr. Pirate," said Monk upon his arrival, trying to ingratiate himself. "How's your collarbone feeling? Is it okay?"

That drew a sharp round of curses from Pirate, aimed point-blank at Monk.

"What did I say?" asked Monk, in an apologetic tone.

That took what was left of the pressure off me.

"This week you don't get to play *your* team. We're choosing up sides among the first ten," said Round Mound, coming through the gate. "No more special treatment for you guys."

Then Pirate popped out his upper teeth and strode onto the court. He played an amazing game with only one good arm, scoring a bunch of baskets and even throwing a few elbows at people.

I don't really remember who won or lost that morning. Probably because it didn't matter much. I just know that our guys mixed with theirs on different teams. I was even Pirate's teammate once or twice. That meant, for a while at least, I had his back and he had mine. And when the games finished, I left there feeling more like a legitimate streetballer than I ever had before.

6

A SUNDAY WITH STYLE

I woke up Sunday morning with my entire body aching from the punishment I'd absorbed playing ball the day before. So I headed down to Astoria Park, looking to jog a few easy laps around its quarter-mile running track and get my stiff muscles to loosen up.

Despite the heatwave, it was prime time there, and the track was packed with people turning laps at different speeds. Angelo was running on the inside lane. He'd been hell-bent on dropping weight before he started at NYU, believing he had a realistic shot at making their basketball team. His pops, a house painter, was there too, speed-walking along the track's outer curve.

"Hello, Paul," said his pops, through a heavy Greek accent and bushy moustache as I stretched on the grass. "Humid day. My crazy son's running in the heat. See you, eh?"

Angelo's pops lumbered past, wearing wooly black socks with white canvas sneakers. Those socks were usually splattered with droplets of paint. I'd joke with Angelo, "I can tell the color of the house he painted yesterday by his socks." Only this morning, his pops's socks didn't have my attention. That's because Wonder Woman was on the track. Angelo and I called her that because she always dressed in the same shiny outfit: red shorts with a blue-and-white top. And since all she did was run at full speed—arriving and leaving that way—she looked like a costumed superhero sprinting somewhere to save the world.

We'd seen Wonder Woman there sporadically for maybe two months. Though she was a major blip on our female radar screen, neither one of us knew her real name or had even managed to say anything to her. Both Angelo and I wanted to meet her badly. It's not that we were tongue-tied. It was just hard to get a word in with a girl running that fast. Besides, she always had on headphones with the music turned up loud enough that you could hear it leaking out. That combination of things made talking to her as difficult as penetrating Superman's Fortress of Solitude.

Out on the track, I watched as Wonder Woman kicked it into extra-high gear. Her long, lean legs gobbled up the ground. She flew past Angelo like he was standing still. Then his head picked up to catch the view from behind. That's when I moved for the water fountain, hoping it might be her last lap. That in this heat, she might actually stop for a drink before sprinting home.

My eyes lit up when she crossed the eight lanes of the track, onto the grass. Wonder Woman was steaming in my direction. I pushed down on the chrome-plated fountain nozzle, creating a streaming arch of water, ready to step aside and let her drink first.

Before the summer started, I had met a girl running here. I got her phone number and asked her out to the movies. She met me at the theater, where I handed her a rose I'd swiped from a bush in somebody's front yard. Halfway through the flick, I'd even slipped my arm around her shoulders. After walking her home, I went to kiss her good night. That's when she freaked out on me, saying, "I didn't know this was a date!" Things like that will shake your confidence to the core. But I was convinced—Wonder Woman couldn't be that oblivious.

As her rapid footsteps approached, I looked straight into her blue eyes. My heart nearly skipped a beat as her mouth opened to speak.

Without breaking stride, she said, "Park water has lead in it. You should only drink bottled."

Then she was gone.

Angelo was suddenly chugging toward me.

"What did she say to you?" he asked, arriving nearly breathless.

"That your friend's getting into shape. But he's way too slow for me," I answered, trying to keep a straight face.

"She did not," he demanded.

"We definitely gave Wonder Woman the right name. All she cared about was keeping me safe," I said, in a disappointed tone.

That's when Angelo's pops came speed-walking past on his next lap.

"Who was that girl?" he asked.

We just shrugged our shoulders in response.

"Hah. She's too fast for you," he said, laughing at our expense. "That's why you're still boys, eh. Not men."

I guess neither one of us could really argue the point. So I took a long, cool drink from that fountain, before wiping my mouth dry with the back of my wrist.

By the time I jogged home that morning, my legs had gotten loose and my stride fell into a good rhythm. So I ran right past our second-floor apartment and motored down to the Proving Ground.

When it comes to streetball, you can never tell about certain yards based on what you see at the moment. Even super-competitive courts are often deserted most of the week. That's because everyone knows to meet there at the right time. They satisfy their basketball jones and then disappear until the following week.

That's how it was at the Proving Ground's courts, where Sunday morning was absolutely dead. And except for some parents pushing their little kids on the shaded swings, the place was empty.

Without a rock in my hands, I stepped onto the main court and could almost feel a game swirling all around me. That's when I began cutting right and left, dribbling an imaginary ball. I'd dart to the corner. Then I'd raise up off my feet and drain a jumper with my wrist and forearm falling into a perfect gooseneck.

I'm not sure how deep I was into that game when I heard a car horn honk from outside the fence. It was Big Reggie sitting in his yellow Cadillac convertible.

"I suppose your shooting percentage is way up today," cracked Reggie in a booming voice. "Come on. Get in. Let's go find us a real game."

"I don't know where there's any good run on a Sunday," I said, feeling slightly embarrassed on the walk over.

"Over by Queens Boulevard," he said, as I opened the passenger door and sat down beside him. Then he broke into a wide grin. "Damn, Paulie. This is a convertible. You don't open the door. You hop in with some style. Do I have to teach you everything?"

"I'll do better. I promise," I said.

"You're probably used to Jumbo's little windup car. This is a Caddy, and you're riding shotgun. Look alive," Reggie instructed me.

There was a hard hat at my feet. Reggie reached over and tossed it into the backseat.

"That's for my job with the phone company," he said.

"Do you climb those high telephone poles?" I asked.

"Hell no. You couldn't get me way up there. Not without a parachute," Reggie answered, as we turned onto the highway. "I do construction for Ma Bell. I ride a jackhammer sucking at an air hose—break up an entire city block of concrete in a single shift. Anyway, what are you studying to be?"

"I don't know. Maybe a teacher," I answered.

"Better work with your brain," said Big Reg. "You couldn't last at construction. Not unless you put some meat on those bones."

We exited the highway at Queens Boulevard and pulled up in front of the basketball courts. There was a game of full court in progress, with one guy standing alone on the sideline and another shooting a basketball on the next court.

"I'm going across the street to park legally. Cops love giving tickets around here," said Reggie. "Go tell that guy on sideline we want to play next game with him."

"You know him?" I asked, stepping out of the car.

"What's the difference?" responded Reggie. "Just tell him."

I approached the guy and said, "I got a friend who's parking. We want to play next game with you."

The guy put his hand beneath his chin, like that statue *The Thinker*, and pondered for a moment.

Then, in a smug voice, he replied, "I don't know. Maybe. I might have to give you and your friend a little test first."

I wasn't sure what to say back, so I kept my mouth shut and went over to shoot the rock with that other dude, who seemed friendly enough.

A minute later, Reggie walked through the gate and headed in my direction. I waited until he was right in front of me before I quietly relayed the first guy's message.

"Maybe? Test?" questioned Reggie, who quickly turned his attention to the guy on the sideline. "Let's have a *test* right now. You two against us. What's the game? Eleven baskets?"

I was surprised when that guy agreed to play and confidently came over. Reggie wasn't raging or anything. But I could see the angered look in his eyes and his massive muscles begin to pump up on their own.

"You shoot for the ball, Paulie," Reggie instructed me. "You guys don't need to warm up or anything? Right? Because I don't."

I stepped to the foul line and drained the shot. It was our rock first. I studied the faces on both of those guys. Neither one looked the least bit worried about us. And I began to wonder how good they might be.

Reggie passed me the ball and said, "Go to the hoop."

He threw a cross-body block, knocking both of those guys into each other before pinning them against the chain-link fence. I dribbled free to the rim and laid the ball into the basket.

"That's one!" shouted Reggie, bouncing back to the foul line for us to check the rock out again. "One to nothing!"

It happened that same way four more times in a row, with Reggie announcing the score to the entire yard. The game on the other court had come to a complete halt to watch. That's when the guy who'd wanted to test us finally walked away.

"Where are you going? It's just five to nothing," said Reggie. "The test isn't over yet. Is it, Paulie?"

"No," I answered, basically on cue.

"And Paulie should know about tests. He's going to be a teacher," added Big Reg.

Then Reggie strode back toward the front gate like a gladiator who'd just finished his business for the day. I put the rock down at the foul line and followed him.

"Sorry to disturb your game," Reggie told the players on the other court. "I know tests are supposed to be taken in quiet. I was too loud."

There wasn't a single complaint.

"You think we passed that test, Paulie? Or was it incomplete?" asked Reggie.

"I think we passed. Aced it," I answered, in a voice loud enough for everyone to hear.

When we reached the convertible on the other side of the street, I made sure not to open the door. Instead, I hopped in with some style.

SELF-REFLECTION: COMMUNICATION SKILLS

Communication is an essential skill mastered by individuals who advance in almost any kind of society. Most streetballers have that quality in their hip pocket. You could hardly get into a game without communicating: Hey, can I play? What are the sides? Who are you going to guard? How many points wins? Ballers also communicate with each other during the middle of a contest, constantly talking on defense in order to make switches and play through picks. In fact, Doc Rivers, who coached the Boston Celtics to the NBA Championship in 2008, said, "If you're not talking, you're not playing defense." Competing and communicating at the same time—that accomplished societal skill is called multitasking. Streetballers are also skilled at a different type of communication: body language. They can read it in their opponents' on-court tendencies—will they go right or left with the ball? They can also project body language, displaying confidence over self-doubt, even when they're not completely sure of themselves.

7

WORRIES AT HOME

Two nights later, I was sitting at the dinner table with my parents in our cramped and steamy kitchen. Mom had made her masterpiece: *pasta aglio e olio*. That's spaghetti without tomato sauce. It's cooked with minced garlic and olive oil. A spindle of it sat twirled around my fork just long enough to shovel into my mouth and wolf it down.

That's when Dad put down his fork for a moment and said, "Your mother and I both have the same question. What's with all these bruises on your arms? Are you playing basketball or training to be a prizefighter?"

I hadn't really noticed the bruises. But as I looked up and down my arms, they were certainly there in every shade of black and blue and purple.

"It's a rougher game at that new park," I answered. "That's all."

"We're just worried about you getting hurt," said Mom, who worked five days a week as a receptionist at a bank. My parents would always joke with each other about getting the combination to the vault so they could sneak inside and roll around on the floor with all that money. "We don't want you being beaten up."

"I can handle myself," I said. "It's not a problem. Really."

"You sure? Because I've seen the guys who play there," said Dad, with a sudden spark to his voice. "There are teenagers. But there are adult men too. And I don't want any man beating on my son. Or else I'll come down to that park, and they'll have to deal with me."

Dad ran the shipping/receiving department for a stationery company. He made sure all the orders were sent out on time from the loading dock where he had seven people working beneath him. He came home every night with stories about how he had to put the hammer down on somebody who'd slacked off. But the one time I went to visit him at his job, Dad's workers pulled me aside and made a point of telling me how much they loved and respected him for having their backs with the bosses. Then I told them Dad was exactly the same way at home: forever on top of me about something but always on my side.

My eyes tilted upward slightly, catching sight of the blades of the ceiling fan slowly turning overhead in our kitchen.

I knew that Dad was serious. If he thought I was being abused, he'd march right onto the court in the middle of a game, willing to fight anybody. I'd fight them all too—Pirate, Snake, Round Mound, even Reggie—if I were forced to. Of course, winning that fight would be a completely different story. It would be okay for me to get my behind whipped in public. But not Dad. I figured he'd never be able to face me or Mom again if that ever happened.

"Maybe we should let him fight his own battles. He's old enough," said Mom, probably sensing Dad's pride and temper about to spike.

"It's just like when you were growing up. Remember you told me about those games at the Educational Alliance on the Lower East Side. The indoor ones with the columns running from floor to ceiling, right on the court. How players tried to knock each other into them," I reminded him. "It's not anything more than that. Just super-competitive ball without a ref."

"All right, but I want you to be careful. And I want to know if any of those men cross the line with you," he said, jabbing a finger into the thick air between us. "Because then I'm going to take matters into my own hands."

"Understood," I said, nodding my head and keeping eye contact with Dad until he went back to his meal.

* * *

That Saturday morning at the Proving Ground was a wild one. The teams were pretty well split up between our guys and theirs. The longtime regulars weren't necessarily trying to intimidate us. Instead, they were too busy beating on each other.

I had Monk and Hot Rod on my squad, along with Surfer Joe and a dude everybody called J-Train, a six-foot-four powerhouse of a subway conductor. J-Train would smile and joke with you all through the warm-ups. But once the game began, he'd fire his elbows at people's jaws like a runaway subway car speeding down the track.

Pirate's elbows were sharp and bony and could cut you. J-Train's elbows were meaty, driven by massive biceps. They were the kind of on-rushing object that could knock you and your front teeth from where you stood today completely into tomorrow.

Gene the Dream took offense at one of those elbows and, for a moment, had J-Train in a wrestling headlock. After that, the pair barked at one another relentlessly up and down the court. I was doing my best to keep clear of that physical war between them. Then Surfer Joe accidentally hit Snake, who was driving to the basket, with a forearm to the chest.

"That's a foul on me," said Surfer Joe, willing to give Snake the ball.

But Snake lashed out at him. "What, are you like these new guys now, trying to be polite? I don't want the foul. Keep the rock. I've got something special coming for you!"

Suddenly, Pirate was trying to play while holding up his pants. The button on his shorts had popped off. Without a hand on his waistband, his shorts were falling down.

"Who's got a safety pin?" asked Pirate, in a tone somewhere between annoyed and embarrassed.

"Why would anyone here have a safety pin," hollered Reggie from the sideline. "You're just too damn skinny to keep your pants up, you old fart."

Everyone was laughing, even those on-court combatants. And just for a brief instant, the tensions seemed eased.

Only Pirate wouldn't step out of the game. He dropped his shorts and played ball in his drawers—a pair of Fruit of the Loom tighty-whities.

Monk turned to me and said, "Pets, there's no way I'm putting a hand on him to play defense. This is insane. If anybody from my real life ever saw me in this game, I'd die."

Pirate played like that for a good five minutes until somebody standing on the sideline produced a pair of swim trunks from his car.

I was impressed that Pirate could completely focus on his game while running around like that in public. In my eyes, it was a total commitment to balling.

"Don't worry, I'll wash them before next week," said Pirate, stepping inside those trunks and tying the drawstring tight. "And there were no skid marks on my underwear. Right?"

That was the last bit of comedy on the court.

With the score tied and just two baskets to point-game, things got nasty again fast.

I glanced outside the fence, and there were my parents. They'd come out of the supermarket across the street pushing a shopping cart full of groceries. They moved slowly up the block with their eyes on the action.

There were three brutal fouls in a row and a lot of cursing in response.

The rock kicked loose as my squad was playing defense, and I grabbed it. There were probably sixty-five feet of open asphalt between me and the unguarded basket at the opposite end. So I took off for it like a jackrabbit on the run.

Behind me, I could hear Gene the Dream and Snake gaining ground with every stride as I dribbled toward the rim. I wasn't worried about them stopping me from making the shot. It was all

"When the only thing you have is a [street] court and a basketball, and you come out a winner. There's no better feeling. It's better than anything. It's better than playing at Madison Square Garden. Here is where [the game] is at its purest form." —God Shammgod, New York City native, streetball legend, and NBA player and coach

about what they'd do to me after the ball left my hand and I needed
to slow up to avoid the fence just beyond the backboard.

A few feet from the rim, with them both breathing down my
neck, I planted my left foot and let the rock gently roll off the
fingertips of my right hand. Then I turned hard to the right without
ever breaking stride, an instant before the two of them slammed into
the fence.

The cheers from my teammates meant the basket was good. My
parents had witnessed the whole thing, reaching the far end of the
block.

"Remember, sometimes the rabbit gets caught," said Gene,
who'd scraped his forearm raw against the fence. "What do you
think happens then?"

Mom and the shopping cart were gone. But Dad remained on the
corner by the traffic light, still observing.

My squad had a stop on defense. Now we had the rock in our
possession, and it was point-game.

Snake had two hands around my waist, unwilling to let me move
in any direction. Then Hot Rod found J-Train down low beneath our
basket and passed him the ball. Snake abandoned me thirty feet
from the hoop to help double-team our big man.

That's when the rock got passed to me, standing wide open. I
knew if I held onto the ball I'd get run over, so I let the shot fly.

It hit the front lip of the rim, bounced against the metal backboard and then fell through the basket.

My teammates were rushing over to give me high fives, while
Pirate was screaming at Snake for walking away from me. But my
eyes had settled on Dad, who'd seen it all from a distance and was
now headed home.

* * *

Almost two hours later, I walked through our front door. Dad,
screwdriver in hand, was fixing the leg on a kitchen chair turned
upside down in front of him. I'd grabbed some bread and sliced
roast beef from the refrigerator before I noticed two sandwiches,
each on its own plate, on the table.

"I figured you'd be hungry, so I made us lunch," he said, raising his eyes up from the chair to meet mine. "I watched you play ball a little bit this morning."

"Yeah?" I said, attempting to sound surprised.

"You handled yourself alright out there," he said. "Of course, your mother's still concerned about you. But I told her that's what streetball is. That you had it under control."

That moment meant more to me than any of the high fives I'd received on the court that morning.

8

STORMING THE SHRINE

Jumbo had a rare Sunday to himself. His wife was taking their children to visit relatives. He was my only friend who was married with kids. In my mind, those situations were for adults. Watching Jumbo's childlike joy on the basketball court, I had a hard time thinking of him shouldering those types of heavy responsibilities.

"Let's take our five and hit The Cages tomorrow," said Jumbo before we left the Proving Ground on Saturday.

"You mean West Fourth?" I asked, instantly in awe of the idea.

The Cages at West Fourth Street in Manhattan is hallowed ground to streetballers. Some of the most competitive games anywhere have been played on that court, including legendary battles between pros and amateurs. It's called The Cages because the tall chain-link fence, along with the spectators lining the sidewalk outside, makes it look like the players and their games are on display in cages.

Without hesitation, we were all in.

"You'll see the difference in the quality of play at The Cages," said Monk, lowering his voice with every syllable and looking over both shoulders. "There'll be no extra nonsense, like here with these guys. Just basketball."

It would be my first time playing there. Angelo and I had passed by The Cages once before. Only the place was packed and we didn't want to wait. Maybe that was our excuse not to take on that kind of competition. But now my confidence was sky-high, and I liked the notion of our squad storming a streetball shrine.

* * *

Overnight there was a rain shower, and the heat wave had broken. We arrived at The Cages in the Brown Betty early in the morning. It was just us there, and we quickly claimed one of the two baskets. I kept pushing my toes into the asphalt, trying to feel the history in the park.

Inside twenty minutes, four guys were standing beneath the opposite hoop waiting for a fifth player to take us on.

No matter where you are, the tenth player into the park is the most important one. That's because no one else can ball until that person shows up. I've been on courts with nine guys waiting for so long we actually begged people walking past to play.

That morning at The Cages, we waited for almost another half hour. The anticipation of playing continued to build inside me, and I had to keep moving to dissipate some of that nervous energy.

Out of nowhere, a tall slender guy walked onto the court, shirtless and without shoes. He was pushing a supermarket shopping cart filled with what looked like all his possessions.

"Look no more. Count me in—I'm number ten," he proclaimed.

That's when he reached into the cart and pulled out a pair of blue-suede Clyde Pumas with the laces already tied, before placing them upon his feet.

The four of us instantly looked at Monk for his reaction in particular.

"I know it's sad," Monk said, sheepishly. "But I still don't want to put my hands all over him to play defense."

"I'll guard him. Let's just play," I said flatly, putting any further delays to rest.

I asked the homeless guy his name.

"Alfonso," he said, making a tight fist and connecting it to mine, exchanging a pound.

A strong smell of sweat wafted from Alfonso's arm pits. But I figured that I'd be in that exact same position inside five hard minutes on the court. So I completely dismissed it.

As a team, we were really on our game that morning, feeding off each other's strengths. Jumbo swallowed up rebounds and loose balls, scoring beneath the basket. Angelo was draining jumpers, and Hot Rod's aggressive hand-checking totally unnerved their ball handler. The opposing team had probably never played together before. And compared to us, they looked like it.

Alfonso was their best player. He had an absolute fire in his belly to compete, badgering his teammates for not hustling enough.

We won the first three games without an anxious moment, and a small crowd had even gathered outside the fence to watch.

"I'll see you boys again sometime," said Alfonso, who bonded more with us than with his own squad. Then he gave us each a half hug to say good-bye. Monk actually lingered in Alfonso's arms the longest, semi-embracing his own fears.

"He's a good guy. He's probably just had some tough breaks," said Monk, as Alfonso pushed his shopping cart out of the park.

As the fourth game began, a bunch of new players assembled on the sideline waiting for next. And one of those guys had a lot to say about our winning streak.

"The only reason you nobodies are still on the court is because the real players aren't here yet!" he barked from the sideline. "You'd have zero chance against a good crew!"

The loudmouthed guy was short, overweight, and looked like he'd never balled a day in his life.

After five minutes of listening to his crap, and with our squad solidly ahead again, Jumbo stopped the game and approached him.

"Why don't you come onto the court and back up your words," Jumbo told the guy. "I'm sure one their players will take a rest to get you in."

"Nah, these dudes are below your squad. Why would I want to get down with them? So you could win another fake game?" he responded with plenty of attitude. "I'll walk out there when it means something. When I've got the proper teammates."

I'm sure all five of us, as well as some of the players on the other team, wanted to slap that guy. But none of us made a move for him, at least not yet.

When the game resumed, I pulled down the next rebound. The guy with the mouth was almost straddling the sideline, with his hands in his pockets. I purposely threw the outlet pass over Hot Rod's head, thinking I could bean that guy with the rock. But Hot Rod took it one giant step further than I'd planned.

He chased after the ball, closing in on that loudmouth. Then Hot Rod forgot all about corralling the rock. Instead, he lowered his shoulder and plowed right through the guy, who probably didn't see Hot Rod coming until it was too late.

Hot Rod absolutely crushed him, and the guy bounced hard off the concrete. The rest of us rushed over to back Hot Rod up. But nobody on the sideline wanted to stand up for that loudmouth.

"Is there something else you want to say?" chirped Hot Rod, standing over the guy.

I was surprised when the guy actually got up from the ground. He didn't say another word and limped out of the park.

That's when the game suddenly ended. The opposing team and all the spectators were in the midst of leaving.

"Where's everybody going?" asked Monk.

"That dude's name is Gary," said one of the players, making his exit. "We know him. Gary's going home to get his hand grenades. So we're all outta here."

The five of us just looked at each other, stunned.

"I can't think of a reason to stay," said Angelo.

Without much conversation about it, we all quickly decided to call it quits for the day too.

On the walk back to the Brown Betty, we spotted a two-story Mickey D's and stopped inside for lunch, maybe just to prove that we weren't running from anybody.

I had a towel draped over my head and was wearing a cutoff sweatshirt. Some little boy, who couldn't have been more than four or five years old, was holding hands with his pops in line behind us.

"Look, Dad," he said, pointing at me excitedly. "It's Luke Sky-walker."

My teammates razzed me about it, but everybody played along for the boy.

"He's on a super-secret mission, kid," Jumbo said, before putting a single finger to his lips to confirm its hush-hush nature.

We all smiled over that and brought our food up to a second-floor table by a big glass window overlooking the street.

Studying the passersby below, Hot Rod said, "If I see Alfonso pushing his cart, I'm going to go downstairs and buy him lunch."

All of us agreed on that and were willing to chip in.

Before we left, I borrowed a pen from a Mickey D's employee who was mopping up. That small boy was sitting with his pops at a table not far from us, eating a Happy Meal. So I went over there and signed his placemat "Luke Skywalker."

SELF-REFLECTION: SOCIAL BONDING

Everyone has experienced that sense of belonging to a group, that "we feeling" usually shared by family members or close friends. It's a sense that together we share a certain set of characteristics, passions, norms, or beliefs. It's an important part of bonding between members of a society. Traveling around New York City as a street-ball squad, we saw plenty of homeless people. I'm embarrassed to say that we would pass right by them, almost without a second thought, as they slept on the street or begged for loose change—as if there were some kind of invisible barrier between us and them. But when Alfonso pulled those sneakers out of his shopping cart and balled against us at West Fourth Street, we began to see him differently. And once he earned our respect on the court, that invisible barrier vanished as we developed that "we feeling" for him. And though we all may tend to judge others at first glance, ballers are fairly open-minded about giving others an opportunity. Their general rule: Prove to me you can play. Prove to me you're somebody.

9

CHRISTMAS IN JULY

On Tuesday night, I got a call from Hot Rod, who was manning his post as a doorman in a Manhattan apartment building.

"You're not going to believe this, Paulie," he said. "I was on Steinway Street headed for the subway to work. There's Pirate coming down off a ladder with a squeegee in his hand. I tell him, 'See you next Saturday morning.' Then he says to me, 'Why don't you come to the park Wednesday night, around five-thirty? We play the same game then.'"

I wished I could have seen my face in a mirror at that moment. Because as the meaning of Hot Rod's words began to sink in, I'm sure I had a smile that suddenly stretched from ear to ear.

"It's like you just told me there's a second Christmas. One I didn't know anything about until just now," I responded.

"I'm going to juggle my shift here so I can make it," said Hot Rod. "Jumbo's coming too. I called Angelo and Monk, but they were hesitating. I'm not talking anybody into playing. They either want to be there or they don't."

"I'll see you tomorrow night," I said, hanging up the phone and then dialing Angelo the instant I heard a dial tone.

"Hi, Paul. How are you?" said Angelo's mom in a Greek accent equal to his pops's. "Come to dinner soon. I'll get my son."

Angelo already knew what I wanted. He picked up the receiver and said, "Because once a week is enough with those lunatics. And I think that's pushing my luck. I don't need to take out any more life insurance."

I could hear the resolve in his voice, so I didn't try to change his mind.

"Besides, my main goal is to make the NYU team in September," said Angelo. "I'd rather blow out my ankle doing that, instead of rolling the dice down there an extra day."

"Monk too?" I asked.

"Yeah," Angelo answered.

"Alright," I said. "Hopefully, I'll see you Saturday."

I understood it clearly. The passion to conquer the Proving Ground simply didn't burn the same inside all of us. More than wanting the guys who played there to recognize my streetball game, I wanted their respect. To be honest, for some unknown reason, I felt like I needed it.

* * *

Early Wednesday, Jumbo stopped by my house. He always took me with him to read the gas and electric meters in the Coca-Cola bottling factory. In their vestibule stood a huge refrigerator filled with free soda. Some of the bottles were too sweet and others not sweet enough—from whenever they needed to adjust the syrup machine. We'd always grab the darkest ones knowing they probably had double the amount of sugary syrup. On that same route, there was a hotdog factory that sold dogs on buns with everything for just fifty cents apiece.

"Too bad Angelo and Monk don't want to play tonight," said Jumbo as we sat on the hood of the Brown Betty, guzzling sodas and munching dogs. "That's the first fracture in our squad."

"They make us choose up sides now at the Proving Ground anyway," I said. "What's the difference if we show up with three or five?"

"I figured the team would last until the end of summer. When school started again and those guys had to study," said Jumbo.

"But not *me*?" I asked, semi-insulted.

"I don't think you're ready to put anything over ball right now, not even school," he replied. "I'm in a hurry. I'll drive you back. I'm making every stop on my route today."

"Since when?" I asked.

"If we're playing tonight, I'm doing a second route for overtime pay. I can't start that till 3 p.m. I need to save all my 'not availables' for then. That'll get me to the park by five-thirty," said Jumbo, opening the driver's door.

"So you're willing to put ball over reading meters," I said, entering on the other side. "Maybe even get yourself fired if you get caught."

"You and me are exactly the same when it comes to this game," responded Jumbo, turning the key in the ignition. "We both want what we want."

* * *

I got to the Proving Ground at a little after 5 p.m. The park was an absolute mob scene. All three full courts had games going on. It was almost entirely teens playing at that time of the afternoon—teens who didn't want to be there at 8:30 a.m. on a Saturday and cut their Friday night partying short.

I sat on the sidelines next to the main court, stretching.

Some kid turned an ankle and needed to step out of the game. Right away one of his teammates pointed in my direction.

"Yo, bro. I've seen you play. We need you," he said to me.

I shook my head no. It was probably the first time in my life I didn't walk onto a court when I was asked. But I wanted to wait until the Proving Ground's regulars arrived.

"Sorry, I'm not even close to being loose yet," I said in excuse, continuing to stretch.

Twenty minutes later, Pirate, Gene the Dream, Snake, and the Round Mound had all walked through the gate.

"Twice a week I've got to see this guy now," Round Mound complained about me. "Hasn't he got a life outside ball?"

"I was about to ask the same thing about you," I immediately shot back at Round Mound, drawing a laugh and a handclap from Pirate.

"We may have to give Paulie the keys to open up the park," said Gene the Dream. "He's always the first one here."

Ten minutes later, after the game on the main court had finished, Snake grabbed a ball and took over one of the baskets. There were at least two full teams ahead of us waiting for next. But somehow, they just seemed to defer to Snake's claim. That's when I realized the five of us were about to play the winners.

The opposing squad was comprised of teen toughs. Two of them wore Oakland Raiders football jerseys with the sleeves cut off. Across the back shoulders their jerseys read "Pain Bringer" and "The Hunter." There was also a short kid with a huge black eye, wearing ripped jeans.

They resembled an urban version of the crew from *Lord of the Flies*.

"See what's written on the back of their jerseys?" I asked.

"You'd have to read it to Pirate," quipped Gene the Dream.

Pirate glared hard at Gene before he said to me, "They can think they're the toughest guys in the world. Good for them. But they're not tougher than us. Nobody is. Remember that."

Those words were ringing in my ears as I threw a series of cross-body block-style picks for Pirate. All he needed was a foot of space to get his lethal shot away. I made sure no one got that close to him whenever the rock was in his hands.

I pulled down a bunch of rebounds too, rifling the ball to Snake, who sprinted ahead of the field for a few easy layups. Then I cut across the key to the hoop, and Gene delivered the ball to me in stride. As three of their players converged on me, I blindly flipped the rock over my head to the Round Mound, who'd been left standing alone beneath the basket.

"What a pass, Paulie!" bellowed Round Mound, after scoring. "You must have eyes in the back of your head!"

He slapped my hand repeatedly, all the way up court.

"Everybody wants to be part of a team. They want to be part of something bigger than themselves. They want to be in a situation where they feel they are doing something for the greater good." —Mike "Coach K" Krzyzewski, who led Duke to capturing five NCAA Men's Basketball Championships and USA Basketball to three Olympic gold medals

Reggie, Jumbo, Surfer Joe, Hot Rod, and J-Train were all on the sidelines now, watching me be an important cog in this streetball squad.

The other team tried to get chippy with us. But we played twice as rough as they did and twice as well. We routed those guys 16–4. And by the end of the game, their toughness turned to sulking, heads down, and arguing among themselves.

I just stood at half-court waiting for the next game to start, feeling like I was on top of the world.

That's when I noticed J-Train walk to the water fountain at the far end of the park. The one that didn't have a huge line of players waiting to use it. Instead, just one guy was leaning up against it, while his two buddies straddled a nearby bench, playing a radio. There was a brown paper bag beneath that bench, and it wasn't hard to figure out that they were there doing business.

From nearly forty yards away, I could read J-Train's lips as he said, "Move. I want to use that fountain."

Gene the Dream had seen it too. He walked three-quarters of the way over there with his arms folded in front of his chest, to be a presence behind J-Train. Streetballers and dealers usually occupy opposite ends of a park. They're basically natural enemies, with each wanting control of as much territory as possible.

I remembered being alone at night, shooting the rock on the one lit court beneath the Triborough Bridge. I went over to the fountain there for a drink. Crouched behind it was a guy shooting up, with a piece of rubber wound tightly around his arm and a syringe in his hand. Neither of us had seen the other until I leaned over the fountain to drink. We scared each other senseless, running in opposite directions. It was a solid month before I'd play on that court alone at night again.

I don't know what would have happened if J-Train hadn't got his way. But that dealer decided to move. Then J-Train took his sweet time and had two or three drinks, probably just to prove his point.

Our squad won the next three games before Snake called it quits for the night, breaking us up. I moved to the benches were Jumbo and Hot Rod were filling out names on a sheet of paper.

"What's that all about?" I asked.

"A dude came by handing these out. There's going to be a street-ball tournament at Steinway Park," said Hot Rod. "How does Angelo spell his last name? I know he's Greek. It must have something like sixteen letters in it."

I was completely stoked at the thought of a tournament. It was like Christmas in July just kept on coming.

Then Pirate walked over and said, "Hey, Jumbo. We need another big body for our team in that tournament. Play with us."

"Sorry," said Jumbo, without a second's hesitation. "I'm already part of a team."

10

SETTING A ROSTER

We needed a name for our tournament team. In the four or so months we'd been playing together as a unit, we'd never once considered calling ourselves anything.

"How about 'Those Five Guys'?" suggested Angelo when we met the next afternoon at the courts beneath the Triborough Bridge.

No one argued against it, so it stuck.

Our only problem was that we couldn't go into a tournament with just five players. Not even if we wanted to. The minimum number of players on the sign-up sheet was eight per team.

There would probably be some leftover players from the Proving Ground. Ones who weren't asked to be on that squad. Only none of us wanted to run with those guys on our team and have people think we couldn't win without them.

Monk knew a college star who was home for the summer.

"He'd probably be the best player in the tournament," said Monk. "We'd have to build our game around his."

"Do you want to ride the bench? Give him *your* spot in the starting lineup?" asked Hot Rod, before Monk shook his head.

Nobody wanted to sit, especially for a stranger.

"I know some guys who were a year behind me at Saint Demetrios," said Angelo. "You've seen them. They've played against us here, under the bridge."

"They're younger and probably only know how to play nice-nice ball," said Jumbo.

"Could you invite them to the Proving Ground on Saturday?" I asked Angelo. "Just to see if they can stand the heat."

In the back of my mind, I could hear the voice of that guy who wanted to test Reggie and me. And I knew I was almost parroting him.

"I'll give them a call and find out," said Angelo.

"And if they don't work out, we can write their names on the roster anyway," said Hot Rod. "They wouldn't have to know."

"That doesn't sound legit," said Monk. "We could get into trouble."

"With who?" mocked Jumbo. "The basketball police?"

* * *

Saturday morning at the Proving Ground, a teenage girl in basketball shorts and sweat socks stood on the sideline. She was there with two guys who I figured were her older brothers, because the three of them looked alike. Between games she came onto the court with them and drained a bunch of jump shots.

"You've got some nice rotation on that ball. But you need more arc," said Pirate, who didn't get a verbal response from her, just a slight nod.

"Stacey's going to be a senior next year," said her biggest brother. "She's a scoring machine. She'll get a college basketball scholarship for sure."

A half hour later, their group of three on the sideline had grown to five. Then it was their turn to play.

The previous game had been won by a squad of Pirate, Reggie, Jumbo, Monk, and me.

"I'd better guard her, Pets," said Monk to me privately. "Can you imagine Reggie, even by accident, knocking her into a fence?"

"She's all yours," I said.

I didn't want to be the one to check her. It was a losing proposition. A guy was supposed to stop a girl on the court. So all you could do was look bad if she scored in your face.

"You're guarding the girl?" Pirate questioned Monk. "She's here to put on a show. Make sure that doesn't happen. I'm not looking to sit next game."

Reggie added, "This is an equal-opportunity country. But that doesn't mean she gets a free pass out here. Make her earn everything."

"Of course," said Monk, his voice cracking a bit.

As the game started, I could see the pressure building on Monk's shoulders. The other squad was intent on working the ball to Stacey. It almost felt like that was the reason they showed up—not to win the game but to prove that she could score here.

Both of Stacey's brothers were setting screens for her. Monk ran into a couple of them. Though Stacey missed her first shot, which rattled around the rim before bouncing out, she canned her second jumper. That bucket diminished our lead to 2–1.

A few possessions later, Stacey was stationed deep in the corner when they worked the ball down low to their tallest player. Monk dropped off her to double-team the ball. It was a split-second defensive choice that most of us would have made. But the rock got kicked right back out to Stacey, probably as planned. Monk sprinted toward her. Only Stacey released a long jumper that caught the front lip of the rim, bounced up to the top of the metal backboard, and then fell home.

"You're supposed to be smart, right?" Pirate chirped at Monk. "A future college boy?"

"He doesn't have any street smarts," added Round Mound from the sideline. "Just book smarts."

She scored once more on Monk, who'd run into another screen set by one of her brothers.

At halftime we held a slim 8-to-6 advantage.

"Paulie, she's yours now. Stop her," said Pirate, as the game paused for both squads to change baskets.

As the second half began, I was shadowing Stacey everywhere. I couldn't hand-check her because I didn't know where I should or shouldn't touch her.

"I had always played with the guys and learned to arch the ball over my brothers, who were a foot taller. I realized early on that the winner wasn't always determined by size and strength, just as later I would realize the single characteristic distinguishing an outstanding athlete from a Hall of Famer was not always physical ability, but desire. . . . I played pick-up games with guys like Magic Johnson . . . with Calvin Murphy and Julius Erving. . . . They were fast, but so was I. They had size, but I had quickness. They had strength, but I had heart." —Ann Meyers Drysdale, Basketball Hall of Famer who recorded the first quadruple-double in NCAA Division I history with double digits in points, rebounds, assists, and steals in a single game

Her biggest brother tried to set a pick on me. But before he could block my path, Reggie blasted him. And I could hear the air leave his lungs as he got crunched.

After that, her teammates focused more on looking over their shoulders for the next potential hit and less on setting screens for Stacey.

The next time Stacey touched the ball, I was right in front of her and completely on balance. Her shoulders squared toward the basket, and I knew she was about to shoot the rock. I almost couldn't believe it, because I was in perfect defensive position. She should have realized that.

As she released the rock, I'd beaten her to the top of her jump. I blocked the ball cleanly with my entire palm, and you could hear the *smack* all over the yard. I sent that ball nearly fifty feet on the fly in the opposite direction. It sailed out of bounds and across the two adjoining courts, all the way to the far fence.

There was a roar of approval from the sideline by the Proving Ground regulars.

"That's called defense, Miss!" shouted Round Mound. "That's what we're known for in this yard!"

I refused to whoop it up with the crowd. Instead, I remained stone silent, looking down at the asphalt, so as not to challenge or embarrass Stacey with any kind of stare. The game had come to a complete halt with the rock at the other end of the park. None of the guys on my squad would make a move to retrieve it, and neither would I.

One of her brothers asked me, "So are you going to get it?"

"Why would I do that?" I answered. "I didn't put up that shot."

Stacey took a first step in the direction of the rock, before that same brother said, "Stay, Sis. I'll get it."

He grumbled and complained all the way over there and back. But wild horses couldn't have dragged me after that ball. It had nothing to do with showing up Stacey. That was *my* block. *My* moment to bask in the glory until someone else returned the rock.

Pirate gave me an approving nod as he calmly chewed on a fingernail.

We pulled away to win that game easily during the second half. Stacey didn't attempt another shot. On their way out of the park, both of her brothers made some remarks into the air about our style of play.

I felt sorry for Stacey. Her brothers had brought her to the Proving Ground for the wrong reason. They wanted to show off how good she was instead of having her game challenged by players who might be better. I wanted to tell Stacey exactly that. But she was walking out of the gate, silent between her siblings. And I understood that right then she didn't want to hear any opinions from me.

Entering through the gate at the opposite end of the park was Angelo's trio of players from Saint Demetrios, almost two hours late. The three of them looked like they were still hungover from Friday night.

"I thought these were supposed to be good Greek boys," Hot Rod chided Angelo, who was already marching toward them. "The ouzo must have been flowing till two in the morning."

"Are you guys going to be dependable?" questioned Angelo.

"Saturday mornings are rough," replied J. K., the one whose eyes were open the most. "Other than that, we're good. I guarantee it."

J. K. was about my height, almost six feet. Only he had a good seventy pounds on me. For somebody that round and stout, he could motor up and down the court surprisingly quickly, resembling a bowling ball with legs and a headband.

Stevie, a tall string bean, lived by the Triborough Bridge. On my walks to the courts there, I'd sometimes see him in his front yard, sunning himself with a mirrored reflector while reclining in a lounge chair. He would start tanning himself in April. By the time June rolled around, Stevie looked like he'd spent time at the equator.

The third kid, a dark-haired weight lifter, was named Bass—like a bass guitar.

Right away, Jumbo asked him, "Hey, Bass. You have any siblings named Viola or Tuba?"

"That would be cool. We could start our own band," said Bass, giving Jumbo a high five, before playing a riff of air guitar.

The three of them played in the next game, and we watched closely. Early on, Reggie put the hammer down, throwing his body around. They reacted like petrified deer, frozen in the headlights of an onrushing Mack truck. Pirate didn't even take them seriously enough to raise an elbow.

"It looks like Sesame Street out there!" sniped Surfer Joe from the sideline. "One of these teams needs to learn its ABCs!"

Their squad got blown out. It was more of a total surrender on the part of the Saint D boys than a defeat. And the three of them walked off the court with their heads hanging down.

"I thought there'd be more fight in them," said Angelo.

"Don't worry. This was perfect," theorized Jumbo. "Now they'll understand their place on Those Five Guys—riding the bench behind us."

11

THE SHERIFF

There would be no major run at the Proving Ground the next Wednesday. That was solely because of the tournament. Both Pirate's team, the Rogues, and our squad, Those Five Guys, had scheduled games.

It was less than twenty-four hours before the tournament began, and we had completely forgotten about uniforms.

"There's no choice now. Just white T-shirts and black magic marker for the lettering," said Angelo, who promised to show up with a bunch of extras in case somebody had brain freeze and blanked on bringing one.

On game night, I walked into Steinway Park and had never seen so many people in one yard before. There were three contests on the schedule, at 5, 6, and 7 p.m. It seemed like every streetballer in western Queens was there to either play or watch.

Pirate's team was up first. The Rogues wore red uniforms with white lettering. The other squad showed up in a similar shade of red. Only that wasn't a problem for real streetballers. The everyday uniforms we recognized were shirts versus skins. But in most yard games, guys just wore whatever they had on, so you memorized their faces and postures on the court. And in the street, those sides could change four or five times a day. Despite all that, guys rarely giftwrapped the rock, passing it to someone on the other team out of confusion.

Just a single ref was hired to officiate the three games. Players understood that he couldn't see everything. That meant there would be a ton of holding and fouling that went uncalled. In my mind, that made the Rogues a heavy favorite.

"When I pull down a rebound, can I raise my arms like this?" J-Train questioned the ref, squeezing the ball in his viselike grip with both elbows extended.

The zebra-shirted ref couldn't have been any taller than five foot three. His soft voice didn't give him much of a presence either.

"As long as your elbows don't contact anybody," he replied quietly.

Round Mound commented that the ref looked like a curly-haired ventriloquist's dummy. And I wondered how long it would be until somebody from the Proving Ground lost his temper, sat that ref on his lap, and made him mouth the desired calls.

The Rogues opposition was huge, in both height and width. I'd heard a trio of them had played college ball in the past. Pirate's squad was severely tested from the start, especially in trying not to commit fouls. Big Reggie got whistled three times inside the first five minutes for obvious hacks. That left him with just three more fouls for the entire game, before he'd foul out.

Eventually, Pirate caught fire shooting the rock. The other team hadn't taken him seriously, probably because of his age. They'd put a low-level defender on him. But right before the half, the *old man* buried six straight jumpers, igniting the crowd and giving the Rogues the lead at the break.

Most of our guys had already arrived. Then Jumbo pulled up in the Brown Betty with bad news.

"I just came from the subway station. I was supposed to pick up Hot Rod. When he didn't show I called his building," said Jumbo, while ditching his work shoes and affixing his sneakers to his feet. "The next doorman on duty didn't show up. Hot Rod's stuck in Manhattan until he arrives."

Losing Hot Rod, potentially for the entire game, would be a big blow.

J. K. was the only one of the Saint Demetrios boys who stepped up and said, "I want to start."

On his ambition alone, Angelo, Monk, Jumbo, and I agreed.

As the second half began, I straddled the sideline, just a few feet from the Rouge's bench, with my eyes glued to every play.

The other team surged back ahead by a slim margin. Each squad played with a take-no-prisoners attitude, and both sides were totally pissed at the ref's calls. The tournament was single elimination—lose once and your team was out. That pushed the stakes even higher. And soon, physical threats against the ref would be muttered out of a half dozen angry mouths.

During a tense stoppage in play, the ref turned to me and said, "You seem to know a lot of these guys. If it gets crazy out here, can you save me?"

"Sure. But exactly who's going to keep *me* safe?" I replied, only half joking.

With just a few seconds left on the clock, the Rogues were trailing by one point. That's when J-Train got hammered down low with the ball. It was an easy call to make and didn't draw an argument.

Gene the Dream called time-out, and the Rogues gathered by their bench in a tight huddle. J-Train, who wasn't a good foul shooter, would have two chances to even up the score. But when the Rogues broke their huddle, it was Pirate who stepped to the foul line instead.

I don't know exactly how, but at that moment neither the ref nor the other team noticed it.

Pirate calmly sank both free throws. And after a wayward inbounds pass by the opposition, the game was over.

As we took the court to warm up for our game, that losing squad began to bitterly complain to the tournament's commissioner, who'd been at the scorer's table keeping the time.

"Totally illegal what they did," protested their captain.

"You're absolutely right," responded the commissioner. "But we can't turn back the clock. Not once the game is officially in the books."

The Rogues were celebrating beside several ice coolers by the park's benches. They wouldn't lie about what they'd done.

"It's not personal," said Gene, after the losers confronted him. "It's just something we got away with. That's streetball."

Then Pirate invited the other squad to share their cooler full of drinks, and several of them actually did, deflating the conflict.

* * *

We were playing the Zoo, Steinway Park's home team. The yard wasn't particularly recognized for its basketball but rather for its bocce—a game mostly played by older Italian men to see who could roll their ball closest to the *pallino*, or smaller bullet ball.

The best streetballer at Steinway Park was a New York City firefighter everybody called Stove. He got that tag because he could heat up a court by nailing jumper after jumper. I'd played with him a bunch of times and basically knew his game inside out. We'd developed a good and competitive relationship, and I considered him a streetball friend. I didn't know, though, that the Proving Ground regulars had a strong beef with him. Stove had gone to the Proving Ground several times over the years and argued with them over his being battered on his way to the hoop and calling fouls.

Stove referred to them as thugs. They'd labeled him a crybaby.

I looked over the Zoo's starting squad. Other than Stove, I didn't see anyone who could put the ball into the basket, maybe even into the ocean on a bad day.

"Let me chase Stove one-on-one everywhere," I told my teammates. "If I can keep the ball out of his hands for a while, who else is going to score?"

J. K. argued with me that he should be the one to guard Stove.

I was totally steamed that J. K. thought he could play better defense.

"I'll tell you what," I snapped at J. K. "First time you think I don't have a handle on Stove, you tap me on the shoulder and I'll hand him off to you."

Just before the jump ball at center court, Jumbo said to me, "I see that look in your eyes. I don't think that kid will be guarding Stove anytime soon."

Stove shook my hand at the circle and said, "Good luck, Paulie."

The Zoo won the opening tap, gaining possession. An instant later, I was more or less standing inside Stove's jock. I was maybe ten inches from his chest, shadowing him everywhere.

His teammates tried like anything to get Stove the rock. But I completely denied him the ball. Almost immediately, the stoked Proving Ground regulars made their voices heard.

"Put him in your pocket, Paulie."

"Stove plays in a soft yard. Show him how we do it."

The Zoo turned the ball over twice, and we scored both times. I was still glued to Stove. The longer he went without touching the rock, the louder and more raucous the crowd got.

Then Round Mound, who was standing on the sideline, shouted in a venomous tone, "You're the new sheriff, Paulie! You've got Stove in the lockup!"

I could see the anger building on Stove's face. And the tighter he got, the easier his next move was to read, allowing me to beat him to that spot.

Our offense was on a roll, scoring on nearly every possession. Angelo's shooting was white-hot, and Jumbo ruled the boards.

It was almost seven minutes into the game, and Stove still hadn't felt the rock. With the score already out of hand, the crowd was completely focused on that one-on-one battle between us.

Stove juked right, and I wouldn't bite at his fake. Then he darted to the left. But I remained his close shadow, denying any potential pass to him.

I understood exactly what I was doing—shutting him out in front of everybody, his friends and enemies. It was all about my ego. I was feeding on everything swirling around me. It might have been totally obnoxious on my part. Only there was something inside me, some deeply competitive streak that wouldn't let me ease up.

Finally, out of sheer frustration, Stove threw a phantom forearm at my chin. I sidestepped it and felt its breeze sail past my face.

The ref blew his whistle, giving Stove a technical foul.

"He's all over me!" Stove raged at the ref.

"But he's not touching you," the ref quickly countered, causing the crowd to scorch Stove even more.

I never took offense at that forearm. I understood what Stove was feeling. I'd taken his pride on what, for us, was a huge public stage.

"It's just a game," I said to Stove, who refused to speak to me.

That's when a member of the Zoo called a time-out. We had more than a twenty-point lead, and the game was essentially over.

When play resumed Stove didn't come back onto the court. He was exhausted, and so was I. A minute later, I waved Bass into the game to take my place.

Stove did return for the second half.

"You guard him now," I told J. K.

"Really? But you're blanking him," he responded.

"I've had enough of chasing him," I said firmly.

For the rest of the game, I didn't go anywhere near Stove, trying not to incur any more hard feelings between us. I'm sure some people thought I was doing him a favor. But I was selfishly doing myself one. I understood he'd eventually touch the ball and score on me. That meant all I could do was backslide in people's esteem. And I was already more than content with the position I'd secured.

We won the game by nearly thirty points, with Hot Rod arriving for the final five minutes or so.

After the game had finished, Pirate whispered to me, "Don't ever think you can guard me like that."

I just nodded.

Then Surfer Joe, who was sitting on top of the benches, lifted up his bottle.

"That was beautiful, Paulie. Somebody get this boy a badge. Because he's the sheriff tonight," Surfer Joe proclaimed, toasting me.

Forty minutes later, after all the adulations had run dry, I walked home drenched in sweat, feeling like I owned the streets of western Queens.

SELF-REFLECTION: THE VALUE OF CONFLICT

Conflict is a major part of life. In fact, conflict is no less important to the formation of a society than cooperation. Streetballers understand this extremely well. Obviously, there's no game without the cooperation of players showing up and agreeing to certain rules. But conflict absolutely dominates streetball. Unlike a battle for a seat on a crowded subway or bus during rush hour, a streetball game has a loser, who normally must leave the court for the sideline. To add to the conflict, streetball is mostly refereed by the players themselves, each with a personal stake in seeing things their own way. But streetballers learn how to deal with those conflicts—often using other important skills they've honed, such as negotiation and conflict resolution. Streetballers don't shrink from conflict. Instead, they perform in the midst of it. And on the days the conflict concludes against them, ballers learn how to shrug it off and move forward.

12

SHELTER FROM THE STORM

I entered the Proving Ground beneath a dark and threatening sky. That's when I noticed her shadow boxing the chain-link fence on the far court. Just last Saturday, right before we'd left the park, she had arrived walking a pair of miniature Doberman pinschers past the kiddie pool and swings. She basically had everyone's attention. Only the dogs had nothing to do with it. She'd been wearing the shortest Daisy Duke cutoffs I'd ever seen, with the white front pockets dangling down beneath the blue denim.

Gene the Dream had immediately approached her. A minute into their conversation, he'd picked both dogs up off the ground and held them in his arms, snuggling his muzzle against theirs. Then he'd offered to drive her and the pooches to Astoria Park.

"It's too hot to walk these dogs on cement," he'd called out to the rest of us, before the four of them hopped into his car. "Somebody's got to be a hero here. I'm going to drive them down to the meadow."

As the car pulled away, Round Mound commented, "That Gene's some smooth talker. I just wonder if his steady girlfriend knows how smooth?"

Now that same girl, sans the dogs and the Daisy Dukes, was here again. Today, she wore sweatpants, martial arts slippers, and boxing wraps around both wrists and knuckles.

There were three of us on the main court as she started over our way.

"You guys know Gene?" she asked, in an aggressive tone.

We nodded in response.

"Well stick around and keep your eyes open," she said, as the wind began to pick up. "I'm going to wipe the floor with him when he gets here."

She said it with such conviction that I absolutely believed her.

Then somebody actually had the guts to ask the question that was probably on all our minds.

"Why? What'd he do?"

She stung the fence with a series of short jabs and replied, "He was supposed to get me a job at his family's construction company. That's what he promised. But he gave me a made-up phone number instead. Now I'm going to pay him back."

Somebody whispered to me, "What do you think Gene got in exchange for that promise?"

I thought she might have overheard that, so I quickly dropped my head and walked to the benches.

Over the next five minutes, most of our guys and the Proving Ground regulars arrived, except for Gene the Dream.

The gathering storm clouds had gotten much darker. Trying to get a game or two in before the rains hit should have been everyone's biggest concern. But not now.

Half of us were praying that Gene wouldn't show up. The other half would have paid money to see him walk through the gate at that moment. Personally, I hadn't decided which of those two camps I was in. Probably a little bit of both.

"Miss, I know you're upset. But could you wait on the sideline?" asked Pirate politely.

"I'm not getting off this court," she said, demonstrating a swift sidekick that would have made Bruce Lee proud.

We were about to move to middle court when a burst of rain sent us running for the shelter of a nearby umbrella of trees. The only holdout was that girl, who stayed on the court firing punches between the drops. And I swore I could see the cool rain raising steam off the top of her head.

That's when Jumbo told everyone, "Let's play beneath the Triborough Bridge, by Crescent Street, where it's low and the rain doesn't get in."

Hungry to play, almost everybody agreed. I was thrilled at the thought of bringing our game to the courts I'd first called my own.

"Hey, Pets," Jumbo said to me, glancing back at that girl still fighting the rain. "She's probably looking for a nice guy. Why don't you ask her out?"

"Honestly, I'd be much too afraid to," I answered, about to take my assigned seat on the hump of the Brown Betty.

* * *

Seven or eight cars pulled up to the pair of courts beneath the bridge, with Brown Betty leading that procession. I was the first one to walk through the gates. It absolutely felt like a homecoming, as if I were the one hosting a big streetball party.

"I've been here a few times," said Pirate. "But it was always just kiddy ball. Nothing challenging."

The images from the first day I'd ever seen him—when he'd singlehandedly destroyed those two obnoxious teens who wouldn't let me into their game—instantly flashed through my mind.

"There's dirt all over the court," said Reggie, looking at his fingertips after dribbling the rock. "It just sticks to your hands."

"That's because the rain never hits the ground here," said Jumbo, pointing to the expanse of roadway approximately sixty feet overhead. "That's the good and the bad of this place."

When I was playing on these courts every day, the dirt got so deep into my hands that it wouldn't wash out. Dad once asked me, "Are you playing ball or mining coal?" A health teacher, who'd noticed my hands at school, had even pulled me aside to inquire, "Do you have soap at your house?"

"How about the *residents* here? Are we going to disturb them?" asked Round Mound, jutting his chin toward a pair of homeless men sleeping in two separate cardboard refrigerator cartons tucked away

"I understood my path and what I meant to the game and what I meant to kids. Not only kids, but individuals around the world. Folks that didn't think that the game was meant for smaller people. For me, I always felt that, tall or small, the game was for all." —Tyrone "Muggsy" Bouges, the shortest player to ever compete in the NBA at five foot three

"In the 80s, Spud Webb [winner of the 1986 NBA Slam Dunk Contest] was the first little guy to be in the NBA. When I was a kid, I'd say, 'Dad what's that little kid doing out there?' 'That's a grown man.' 'Why is he so little?' 'You're going to be little just like that. So take notes.'" —Nate Robinson, five-foot-nine pro point guard, college football player, and winner of the 2006 NBA Slam Dunk Contest

beside the huge cement pylons of the bridge. "Are they both named Maytag? That's what the signs on their houses say."

"I know. It's sad," said Monk.

"Remember, that could be any of us one day," said Pirate, before popping out his upper teeth. "But it isn't today, so let's play ball."

The park wasn't designed for the type of take-no-prisoners ball that was about to be played there. The baskets and backboards weren't attached to the fences. Instead, they were connected to a metal pole cemented into the ground at the edge of the court.

"How much give is in this pole?" asked Reggie, who then lowered his shoulder and purposely rammed it.

That basket and pole must have shook for a half minute from the blow.

"Hit that going full speed, and you'll feel it," concluded Big Reg.

Angelo, Monk, Hot Rod, Jumbo, and I exchanged cautious looks with one another. We'd danced around those poles plenty of times with no one ever crashing into them, accidentally or otherwise. But we understood that today could be different.

Sides were chosen, and the games started up.

For the first time, Angelo and Pirate actually played together. The two of them simultaneously caught fire shooting the rock. The bolts securing both rims there were loose. Any jumper that found the front lip of the iron, instead of bouncing away, would fall home.

That was all the edge those two sharpshooters needed. They're squad easily won the first four games. They didn't get challenged until a team of totally thug-minded defenders led by Reggie, Hot Rod, and Snake began pounding them. In response, Pirate retaliated by throwing a wild elbow at nobody in particular. It sliced through the air, connecting with nothing but that metal pole, producing a high-pitched *ping*.

Luckily, Pirate had just hit his funny bone. He danced around the court, somewhere between tears and laughing, with everyone else settling clearly on the side of laughter.

That one morning, I didn't mind being on a losing team. I just sat on one of the concrete benches, soaking in the action. This yard had spawned the roots of my game. Now I was returning, surrounded by legitimate streetballers who treated me as one of their own.

A kid named Beans, who I used to ball with all the time, got into one of the games. I'd once played touch football in the street with Beans during a snowstorm. At least, I thought it was going to be *touch* football. I took my first step off the line of scrimmage, and the kid blasted me into a snowbank.

"Sorry, Paulie," he'd said, as I spit ice from my mouth. "I figured with the snow covering the concrete, this was tackle."

Beans wasn't much of a basketball player. You could measure his ability to jump in dust particles. But he had a natural football mentality, being built solidly with a low center of gravity. That helped him to survive the ultra-physical style of play on the court.

"You see my glasses, Paulie?" asked Beans at the conclusion of a game. "I left them on one of these benches."

"I didn't notice," I replied.

"Could any of these lunatics on the court have swiped them?" he asked.

"I wouldn't say that too loud," I advised him.

"My parents are going to kill me. It'll be the second time I've lost them this year," he said, suddenly stressed to the max.

That's when we saw one of those homeless men who'd been sleeping walking out of the gate wearing Beans's specs.

Beans went charging over there and took them back.

Later on, Pirate approached that homeless guy. He pulled a wad of bills from his pocket and handed him a $20.

"That's for you and your partner," said Pirate, pointing at the other one who was still asleep. "Get yourselves a decent meal."

"I left my wallet at home or I'd add to that," interjected Round Mound.

When the games finished that morning, there was still no sign of Gene the Dream.

"I wonder if he showed up at the Proving Ground after we left?" pondered Jumbo aloud.

"If he did, we'll probably hear the headline on the six o'clock news—'Woman Beats Man into Coma,'" added Snake.

Just beyond the shelter of the bridge, raindrops ricocheted high off the concrete, splattering in every direction. Everyone else seemed to be complaining about it. But I thought it was absolutely beautiful. To me, it looked like a street flooded with shining diamonds.

"You don't live far from me, Paulie. I'll drive you home," said Snake.

I had to lower my head and fold up my legs to fit in the passenger seat of Snake's Corvette.

That Stingray practically hugged the ground, cornering tight turns like it was an extension of the road. Like it was an extension of Snake's will.

I hadn't been in any hurry for a driver's license, considering my parents didn't even own a car. But that sleek ride through the rain had my adrenaline pumping.

"Watch me stop on a dime, right at the crosswalk," said Snake, with supreme confidence. "There, not an inch over."

Snake commanded all that horsepower beneath the hood with a single relaxed hand on the steering wheel and a second on the stick shift. After witnessing that, it was easy to understand why, despite his diminutive size, Snake believed he could accomplish anything on the basketball court.

13

ROUND TWO

Tuesday night brought second-round tournament games for both Those Five Guys and the Rogues. Again, Pirate's squad was slotted to play in the contest directly before ours. The Rogues took on a team of athletic giants. Their opposition was a mix of high school all-stars and beefy college-aged ballers.

As I watched the warm-ups, I knew the Rogues would have their hands full. The other team was running a layup line, and nearly every dude rocked the rim with a dunk. The backboard shook, and before it stopped, another of their players flushed one down with authority. It went on that way for several minutes, as if that particular basket were built on a fault line and suffering the aftershocks of an isolated earthquake.

The Rogues weren't blind to it. The starting lineup of Pirate, Reggie, J-Train, Snake, and Gene the Dream all had their game faces screwed on tight.

"Maybe that girl from the park, my personal stalker, assembled this team," said Gene. "Maybe this is another way she wants to kick my ass in public."

That ref from the week before—the ventriloquist's dummy who'd let Pirate sneak to the foul line—was gone. He'd been replaced by a tall, slender dude who looked like he had ice water in his veins. Some players recognized him from refereeing local high school and college games. So the Rogues were probably going to be forced to play by the rules.

Despite all of that, the Rogues held a 10-to-8 lead early on. Then the other team, which actually had a coach, began to full-court press, pushing the Rogues to play faster and faster.

Pirate's squad could do a lot of things well. But dribbling the rock under intense defensive pressure wasn't among them.

Their game fell apart fast after Gene and Snake couldn't get the ball past half-court on three consecutive possessions facing the opposition's press. Then Reggie got called for a pair of quick fouls. By Reggie's overly physical standards, he'd barely grazed anyone.

"Damn, Ref. I can't even breathe on them?" argued Reggie in frustration. "I used mouthwash this morning."

In a flash, the Rogues were down by eight points.

Pirate couldn't shoot the Rogues back into the game because his ball handlers couldn't get him the rock.

The Rogues tried to roughhouse. Only the other team had real legs. It's hard to hit what you can't catch. Despite their determination, Pirate's crew didn't have the athletes to compete against an organized herd of gazelles able to play the game at a high level.

By halftime it was a blowout. Pirate stewed all through the break, and the rest of the Rogues argued with each other over their poor play.

"Don't turn your back while you're dribbling," Gene lectured Snake. "That's when they attack you from the weak side."

"I don't turn my back to anything," snapped Snake. "And I don't have a weak side."

The game wasn't competitive during the second half, and the Rogues' deficit widened. Proving Ground regulars weren't good at handling a loss, especially to strangers. But they were even worse at accepting a beat-down.

With just a minute or two left on the clock, the other team's biggest player blocked Pirate's shot. That's when the old man lost it. He fired several punches into the Big Man's midsection. Only those blows didn't have the slightest effect.

In response, the Big Man extended a straight arm onto Pirate's shoulder, keeping him just out of reach, with Pirate now punching the air between them.

It almost looked like a cartoon.

"I'm not fighting somebody the same age as my pops," said the Big Man, who seemed more amused than angry.

The crowd thought it was hilarious. So did almost everyone on the court, except for Pirate, whose face was beet red with anger.

Gene, Reggie, and the opposing coach led Pirate away. The ref calmly ejected him from the game. And with the Rogues about to be eliminated from the tournament, the commissioner didn't need to suspend Pirate.

A few minutes later, after the game had ended, Pirate's anger subsided and he was back on planet Earth. He shook hands with the winners and even laughed at himself.

"It's nothing personal," Pirate told the Big Man. "That was just my temper talking. My pride can't accept that kind of beating at ball."

I was probably one of the few observers who didn't find any part of that scrap amusing. Maybe because I'd already been through it with Pirate, for what seemed like no reason. Or maybe because it felt like eventually somebody was going to get really hurt.

The Proving Ground regulars emptied out of Steinway Park in a hurry. They weren't about to hang around after a crushing defeat. I'd have done exactly the same. I had fantasized about meeting the Rogues in the tournament's championship game. But that dream was dead. Now it was Those Five Guys' turn to stay alive.

* * *

We'd drawn the team that captured last year's championship. Surprisingly, they weren't any bigger or stronger than our players. We were mostly forced to battle squads with huge height advantages over us. So looking at them gave us an extra spark of confidence.

"You know they play like a team," said Jumbo, just before the tip-off. "They don't have enough of a physical edge to be selfish out there."

"And they've been playing together longer than we have," said Monk, as we walked onto the court.

Angelo and Hot Rod both glared at Monk.

"Are you a member of *their* fan club or *ours*?" questioned Hot Rod.

"Ours," replied Monk instantly. "Definitely ours."

Throughout most of the first half, our shooting touch was frigid. As a team, we hadn't endured a collective ice age like that in a long time. Maybe it had something to do with nerves, going up against the defending champs. But the rest of our game fell perfectly into place. We rebounded, played D, and swung the ball to the open man like clockwork. We looked and felt like the better team. Only our shots refused to drop.

Angelo pulled the trigger on a corner jumper. The rock rolled around the rim three times before it spun out.

"There's an invisible lid on that basket," grumbled Angelo.

Jumbo missed a short shot. I'd boxed my man out and grabbed the bound. I had an easy put-back from beneath the basket at point-blank range. But that rock rattled inside the rim and wouldn't fall. It came right back to me for a second try. The odds of me missing two of those in a row were probably 100–1 against. Only that's just what happened.

On our next possession, Monk released an open jumper. Fighting for position, I buried a hip into my defender. I listened for the sound of either the ball swishing through the net or clanking off the rim. Neither occurred. Instead, I heard a dull *thud*. That's when I looked up and saw the rock wedged between the backboard and the basket.

"You couldn't do that again if you tried for a week straight," Jumbo barked at Monk, as the ref awarded the opposition the ball.

Despite those glaciers rolling off our fingertips, we went to the half trailing by just six points.

"We should be trouncing these guys," said Hot Rod. "We make a third of those shots and we're way out in front."

"I think someone should explain to [kids] that it's OK to make mistakes.
That's how we learn. When we compete, we make mistakes." —Kareem
Abdul-Jabbar, New York City native, Rucker Park participant and historian,
and six-time NBA champion

Then Jumbo put his arm around Angelo and said, "Clear your mind of all the outside noise. Just concentrate on your mom's pork chops and french fries. How if you don't start making shots, the other squad's going to show up at your house to eat your dinner."

That threat must have made an impact. Because a few minutes into the second half, Angelo swished a shot from twenty feet, with a defender draped all over him. He buried his next two jumpers as well.

Nobody's exactly sure what causes momentum to swing in a basketball game. Or when an ice age will begin to thaw. But Angelo's sudden hot hand seemed infectious, and the rest of us began sinking baskets too.

Inside two minutes left to play, we surged to the lead. Then Hot Rod fouled out of the game. J. K. wasn't there. He'd gone on vacation with his parents to Greece. So Bass came off the bench to take Hot Rod's place.

"Just hold onto the ball. Don't try to be a hero," Jumbo instructed him. "We're setting Angelo up to shoot. He's in rhythm right now."

"I hear you," said Bass, before his girlfriend on the sideline gave him a kiss for good luck.

The opposition's defense backed way off Bass, who was standing ten feet past the top of the circle. They figured he wasn't coming in cold from the bench to hoist shots. And they should have been correct.

With less than thirty seconds to go, Angelo was being hounded by a double team, as we protected the rock and a one-point advantage.

Monk passed the ball to Bass, alone at the top of the key.

"Shoot it," screamed somebody on the other team.

I could see Bass's face go blank in confusion, an instant before he released the shot.

The rock hit nothing—not the rim or the backboard. It just sailed out of bounds, and the opposition took possession.

We didn't need to waste time being mad at him, especially with a lead still to protect. But in the waning seconds, one of their players threw up an off-balance prayer in heavy traffic. The shot laid on the

rim and then trickled through the basket, booting us from the tournament.

Angelo was about to unload on Bass. His mouth opened wide.
But before his first fiery word escaped, Bass's girlfriend spit some
venom of her own.

"What the hell were you thinking?" she screamed at Bass. "If
you're ever walking over a bridge, remind me not to yell 'Jump!'
Because you just might do it!"

In the face of that kind of embarrassment, the rest of us just bit
our tongues and left Bass alone. We disappointedly slapped hands
with the other squad and quickly found the exit.

14

THE LETTER

I felt left out because Angelo and Monk were constantly talking about the freshman classes they were going to take in September. They'd carefully plotted their plans for college, while I'd basically chosen a school on a whim and only got accepted due to low enrollment for that coming semester. Back in July, they had both received letters from their schools listing all the possible classes and schedules. My letter didn't arrive until the second week of August.

I didn't have that letter open for more than a few minutes before I was on the phone with Angelo.

"How many credits do you think I can handle?" I asked, with the pages spread out in front of me on the kitchen table.

"I'm taking eighteen. That's six classes," answered Angelo, who had been a top-notch student in high school.

"That sounds like a mountain of work. My last math class was a joke. The descriptions of the ones here look serious," I said, considering I'd graduated without taking a single statewide exam. "Maybe I'll just go for twelve credits and have Fridays completely free."

"Then you can have a full day to prep for Saturday morning at the Proving Ground," said Angelo, in a pointedly sarcastic tone. "You can probably pick up three credits for your personal study of urban pirates. Call it life experience."

I didn't take any offense at that because Angelo was absolutely right. I was interested in putting together a schedule that left me time to ball in the street.

Suddenly, that summer morning took an extra shine.

As I hung up the phone, out the kitchen window I saw a girl on the other side of the block. She was on the second-floor balcony, painting the wrought iron fence that surrounded it. Only she might as well have been painting the *Mona Lisa*, because I couldn't take my eyes off her.

Her blonde hair was tied up in a red bandana, and her clothes were covered in streaks of paint. She looked to be about my age. I was fairly sure I'd seen her face before. Maybe as a kid. But she had definitely grown up since.

Every few minutes or so, I'd go back to the kitchen window to check on her progress. All the while, my brain was devising a plan to meet her. I didn't consider it cool to open the window and call out to her across the way. The best idea I came up with was to knock on her front door and ask to borrow a paint brush. I was actually going to do it. Only the next time I looked, she was gone.

A moment later, through the alleyway beside her house, I saw her walking toward the top of the block. I bolted for the door in hot pursuit. I grabbed a basketball on the way out, just to have something in my hands.

She was walking westward, in the direction of Astoria Park. I kept a good three-quarters of a block behind her, trying to figure out where she might be headed. I only knew that she was walking fast and with a purpose. Eventually, she turned into the backyard of the local elementary school, PS 122.

I figured fate was on my side because there was a pair of basketball hoops there. She stopped at the school's back door, where a bunch of parents had gathered.

A couple of junior high–aged kids were shooting at one of the baskets.

"Hey, how come all those people are waiting by the door?" I asked the kids on the court.

"Summer camp lets out in a few minutes, at three o'clock," one of them replied.

That's when I took the ball in my hands and purposely dribbled it off my sneaker. It rolled through the gate separating the hoops from the school's back door. If I'd been bowling, it couldn't have been a more perfect strike, stopping right at her feet.

She bent down to pick it up as I jogged over.

"Thanks," I said, as she handed me the ball. "Don't you live around the block from me? On Twenty-Seventh Street?"

"Sure, I remember you," she said, smiling. "I haven't seen you in a long time. Here to play ball?"

"Yeah. How about you?" I asked.

Her name was Mia, and she was there to pick up her eleven-year-old sister. Fate continued to be on my side, as I glanced at the T-shirt Mia was wearing. It read "Baruch College."

That was the school I was about to attend.

"I'm starting Baruch in September," I said.

"It's a great school. You'll like it," said Mia. "I'm actually a freshman there too. But I got a chance to take a class there this summer."

"Thing is, I don't know much about the campus and the different buildings," I said, as her sister emerged from the doorway, along with a bunch of other kids. "Would it be okay if I knocked on your door some time? Get a few insights from you?"

"Not a problem," Mia said.

After Mia and her sister left, I settled at the open hoop and shot the rock for maybe twenty minutes. I felt like I'd just scored the winning basket in a big game. I was proud of myself, basking in the glory of a patchwork plan that had remarkably come together. I felt almost superhuman, like I could accomplish anything.

I didn't know much about the lottery, except that my parents played it every week without success. But right at that moment, I felt like I could predict the winning numbers.

* * *

That Saturday at the Proving Ground was incredibly physical. Players were pounding each other left and right. The yard resembled the Roman Colosseum more than a basketball court. And for the most part, the participants were willing to fall on their swords before ever uttering the word "foul."

Angelo and Monk, sensing the mood of the morning, had smartly made early exits. I wasn't that bright.

Pirate was pissed about Wednesday night's tournament drubbing. His elbows were working overtime, slashing at anyone who blocked his path to the rim. Thankfully, Pirate was on my squad, though I still made sure not to get in his way.

With our team short of height, I guarded J-Train. He was too big and powerful to push and shove against. So I took the path of least resistance. I tried sticking to him like flypaper, with my relaxed body glued to his. It worked, and J-Train was having a terrible time trying to shake loose.

"You're like my damn shadow," complained J-Train. "You gonna follow me to the toilet too?"

Despite his frustration, J-Train didn't hammer me with an elbow. I was playing him cleanly, and he responded the same way with me.

Some dude stepped off the handball courts and into our game, taking somebody's place who'd had enough. I could tell by the way he moved that he hadn't played much ball. But he must have been watching me stick to J-Train, because he tried doing exactly the same to him.

Without a second's hesitation, J-Train throttled the dude by the throat and body slammed him to the concrete.

I could feel the hurt inside my own bones just watching that.

"Don't you ever believe you can do me that way," J-Train hollered, standing directly over him.

Eventually, guys helped that dude to his feet before he limped out of the park. Then I assumed my place next to J-Train, this time leaving an open space between us.

"It's one thing for you to guard me close, Paulie," said J-Train, his eyes still glowing with anger. "I'm not about to have some handballer belly up to me."

That's when I realized it was all about perception. J-Train could stomach me stopping him because I had a rep as a defender. But he wasn't going to be challenged by someone who'd barely played the game thinking he could do it too.

The violence didn't end there.

Two minutes later, Pirate and Jumbo exchanged a hard bump. Pirate responded with a flurry of wild punches at Jumbo's head. Jumbo tied him up inside his octopus-like arms. But Pirate broke free and grabbed a small ice chest off one of the benches before trying to crack Jumbo's skull open with it.

Jumbo stalked out of the yard, cursing at Pirate.

"You need help! Serious help!" screamed Jumbo, heading toward the Brown Betty. "You're going to kill somebody over basketball one day."

It was all five or six guys could do to restrain Pirate, who had totally lost it on the court for the second time inside a week.

That fight signaled the end of the games that morning. Nobody had a taste for playing after that, including me. And I began to worry, on a really bad day, just how far Pirate could go in losing his temper.

SELF-REFLECTION: DEFUSING CONFLICT

Conflict resolution is a highly valued social skill. It's something streetballers absolutely understand. After all, not every intense disagreement, on either the court or the sideline, ends in an all-out brawl with blows exchanged. Because if it did, there would be very little basketball played. Nearly every game would have to be halted before the final score, and most of the players would leave dissatisfied—with their streetball appetites unfulfilled. So streetballers learn how to defuse tense situations. They understand that people have different goals and personality traits. In the midst of this physical and often aggressive game, ballers learn to use their words. They generally know how to both listen and speak, using tone of voice, body language, and distance from someone who is angered as means of cooling a confrontation. It is a skill that serves ballers far beyond the boundaries of a basketball court—at home, school, and work and in personal relationships.

15

BALLERS VERSUS BADGE

On Monday, I decided to walk up to the public library on Steinway Street. The idea of taking a legitimate math class had me nervous. My last math course in high school wasn't for students headed to college. It mainly consisted of measurements—calculating square yards, applying the metric system, and using tools like rulers and micrometers. The only higher math I knew was figuring out the perfect angle to execute a bank shot off the backboard.

Two blocks from my destination, I saw Pirate across the street, busy cleaning the windows of a pizzeria. I could have stayed on the other side and passed by unnoticed. But I crossed against traffic to talk to him.

Before I could say anything, he saw my reflection in the glass as I came up from behind.

"You looking for work, Paulie? Besides this route, I got a business cleaning offices at night. Surfer Joe does one for me. But you can't be lazy. Things have to be cleaned right. It's my reputation on the line," said Pirate, without ever turning around or interrupting his long strokes with the rubber squeegee in his hand.

"Nah, I'm okay. I've got to get ready for school. That's why I'm going to the library," I said.

"That's smart. Education's more important, even more important than ball. Remember that," said Pirate, connecting his fist to mine. "You saw what happened on Saturday?

"You mean with you and Jumbo?"

"He's not innocent in that thing," said Pirate, walking toward his car, which was double-parked at the curb, for a fresh roll of paper towels. "He hit me hard before I got started with him."

"You don't think you were over the edge?" I asked, couching my words carefully. "Just a little bit."

"I get angry fast," Pirate replied. "I didn't have it easy growing up. You know I have trouble reading right? That's one thing I wished I'd learned better in school."

"I didn't know," I said. "But you run a business. How'd you get a driver's license?"

"I memorized how the answers looked in the book—the driver's manual," he said. "Maybe one day I'll take a reading class. Get better at it. You're never too old to learn. You got a license?"

"No, not yet."

"I can teach you, Paulie," said Pirate. "It's not hard. And I'm a good teacher. I taught my daughter."

Then, from over my shoulder, I heard the most obnoxious voice I could ever imagine.

"If that vehicle with the ladders belongs to one of you, move it now or else," said a traffic enforcement agent, striding toward us.

He had to be in his early thirties. There was a sneer on his face, while his shirtsleeves were rolled up so high it almost looked like he was wearing a tank top. I wasn't sure how to react or what kind of power he wielded. But that shiny badge pinned to his chest didn't stop Pirate from speaking his mind.

"Listen, I'm working here. Why are you hassling me? I'll be done with this stop in a minute, and then I'll move the car," said Pirate, in what for him was a measured tone.

Then that traffic agent quickly raised the stakes.

"Did I ask you for a story? Or did I tell you to move the car?" he responded, closing the gap between Pirate and himself until they were just a few feet apart.

"I like the way you've got those sleeves rolled up. Those are some nice muscles," said Pirate, with each word becoming more pointed. "Are you trying scare somebody? You think you're a tough guy?"

I jumped in front of Pirate, as if I were boxing him out from getting a rebound on the court.

"I'll move the car myself. Don't worry about it," I said, with Pirate trying to push his way past me.

That bigmouth with the badge flapped his gums again.

"Go ahead. Come at me. Get locked up for being double-parked," he said.

"I been to jail plenty of times," countered Pirate. "You'd be worth another trip."

I had visions of Pirate and me both being arrested—of my parents refusing to bail me out of jail, just to teach me a lesson.

That traffic agent didn't have a gun, just a radio holstered on his hip. I watched him drop his hand on top of it, like he was about to call for reinforcements.

It was a bad position for me to be in, semi-sandwiched between them.

"Write the ticket if that's what you're going to do," I said. "Just step back."

Thankfully, the officer finally moved in the opposite direction. Then he started to write in his ticket book.

"You're a troublemaker," he told Pirate, placing the ticket beneath one of his wiper blades.

"And you're a punk, first-class," retorted Pirate. "I can pay that ticket all day long. I work two jobs to your one."

"Better watch yourself. Those ladders strapped to the top of your vehicle are probably against the law," said the agent, as he made his way down the sidewalk checking parking meters.

"I guess you wanted to be a cop but they wouldn't take you," taunted Pirate. "Go away, before I put money into every expired meter on the block. Then you won't have a job."

"If you lived in cities like Detroit, Chicago, Los Angeles, New York, Philadel-phia . . . [a]ll of us, the first time we touched a ball was outside on the playgrounds. . . . I enjoyed it so much, I met so many good people over the years playing streetball, had so many good friends. . . . But like I said, we had big battles on the playground, just all-out battles where everything we did was just go at one another. So for me, I had to be on top of my game every single game. It kept the city alive." —Rafer "Skip to My Lou" Alston, street-ball legend and NBA point guard

I was breathing easier as the distance between them grew. But rolling the dice on being handcuffed and hauled off to jail wasn't what I'd had in mind when I stopped to talk to Pirate.

"You want some pizza, Paulie. I'll pay," said Pirate.

"No, I need to get to the library. I'll see you Wednesday night," I said, making my exit.

Two blocks later, I entered the library. Staring me in the face, thumbtacked to a bulletin board next to the circulation desk, was an orange flyer that read, "Classes for Adults: Reading and Writing."

On a table right beneath it, there was a whole stack of those same flyers. I took one, carefully folded it into quarters, and put it in my pocket.

* * *

Walking home from the library, I stopped at the top of Mia's block. Angelo thought I should wait at least three days before knocking on her door. It was almost 2 p.m., just about an hour short of that three-day mark. I figured she'd be at home, waiting to go pick up her little sister from summer camp. So I swallowed hard and started toward her house.

I was carrying two math textbooks I'd just checked out of the library. I knew that looking studious probably wouldn't hurt my cause.

There was a bell, but a knock with my knuckles felt more personal.

Almost on cue, Mia answered the door. Then we sat on her front stoop and started talking about school.

"If you catch the subway right at the station, it's no more than a twenty-minute ride into Manhattan," said Mia, as the sun broke through a bank of clouds, turning her hazel eyes a lighter shade of brownish green. "I usually leave my house about an hour before class starts. Do you know what classes you want yet?"

I was prepared and had perfectly anticipated that question.

"I saw one on the list about the movies—'Film as a Reflection of Society,'" I answered, before tapping on the textbooks in my hands. "Sounds like a lot more fun than higher mathematics."

"Maybe eating popcorn's part of the final," she said with a widening smile, evoking the same reaction from me. "I noticed that class too. I wouldn't mind taking it. I just don't know if it fits my schedule."

"One of the films on its syllabus is playing just a few blocks from the school," I said. "I'm going to see it on Friday night. You want to go with me?"

"Sure," Mia said, studying my eyes closely.

Then Mia's mouth opened to say something more. Only she hesitated and never actually did. I think at that exact moment, she understood the chess game I'd just played. Perhaps in her brain she had even revisited all the moves I'd made.

In any case, she didn't seem to mind.

"Pick me up at seven o'clock," she said. "I'll see you then."

I had left the stoop, and Mia was headed back toward her door when I called her name.

The last time I'd been to the movies with a girl, she had no idea that it was date and was shocked out of her skin when I tried to kiss her goodnight. My pride couldn't take another disaster like that.

"By the way," I said to Mia, "in my mind, this is a date."

"That's what I was thinking too," she said, seemingly amused as she stepped back inside her house.

16

THINKING FORWARD

At around 5:30 that afternoon, Angelo, Monk, and I met at the courts beneath the Triborough Bridge to play round-robin one-on-one. I told them all about Pirate's near brawl with that obnoxious traffic agent. Then I took kudos from them both for my pursuit of Mia.

"It's like you're a spy from that TV show *Mission Impossible*," said Angelo. "Tracking strange girls through the streets. Then showing up at their house."

"Not James Bond?" I asked, hoping for a little more prestige.

"No, 007 doesn't carry math textbooks as cover," Angelo countered, as we warmed up.

"It's a good catch though, Pets. You told yourself you wanted to meet her, and you made it happen. That's how the world works," added Monk, tucking his T-shirt into his shorts. "Now are you going to take that same determination and make your college basketball team?"

"I can't say I'm possessed by that," I answered. "I'm getting enough run playing streetball."

"You need a step up in class, Pets," said Monk, taking the court against Angelo in a one-point game, with me awaiting the winner. "Real competition against serious players. Not hoodlums playing bully ball."

Angelo buried a jumper in Monk's face, and I came onto the court.

"How do you think I should hand Pirate that flyer about reading classes?" I asked a half second before Angelo drilled another shot, sending me back to the sideline.

"You think he's going to be happy about that," said Angelo. "He might use it to hold a serious grudge against you."

"That's true. There's no predicting his reaction," said Monk, shoveling Angelo the ball and getting into a defensive stance. "But I would certainly do it in private. Remember, he may have trouble even reading the flyer."

That was something I hadn't considered.

"It'll be interesting to see how Pirate and Jumbo get along on Wednesday night," I said. "If they have another blowup."

"Call me and give me a full report because I'm not coming," said Angelo, after nailing another shot and turning Monk and me into his personal merry-go-round, walking on and off the court.

"I won't be there either. Or on Saturday," said Monk. "I leave Sunday morning for college in Pennsylvania. It's orientation week for freshmen. I'm not going to risk an injury playing with those guys. I'm focused on making my school team."

"Same for me," said Angelo. "I'm interested in wearing my school's uniform. Not a hospital gown."

Deep down, I'd known the team we'd assembled had an expiration date. That September and school would ultimately break us apart. But I didn't believe we'd splinter in mid-August, especially over the fear of getting hurt. Because fear had absolutely no place in climbing the streetball ladder.

It was disheartening to hear. But I pushed it out of my mind and balled.

Angelo was white-hot and wouldn't miss, even after Monk and I got super-serious about stopping him. He'd dropped fifteen pounds over the past month, eating nothing but grilled chicken, tomatoes, and grapes.

"That's what I mean by commitment, Pets," said Monk. "Angelo gave up all his favorite foods to be in better shape and chase the college ball dream."

The three of us went at it for probably forty fast-paced minutes without a break. Angelo wouldn't even hit the fountain, gauging his water intake with his meals.

"You really need to drink more, Ange," said Monk. "Don't worry about water weight. You need to keep hydrated. It's hot out here."

Two minutes later, Angelo passed out. First his cheeks turned beet red. Then his eyes closed, and down he went, lucky to not hit his head on the concrete.

As soon as we threw water on Angelo's face, he instantly came back around.

"Don't mention this to my parents," said Angelo, between gulps at the fountain. "My mother will cook a six-course meal and make me eat every bite."

After that, Monk and I made sure to walk Angelo home.

* * *

The next day, I had that pair of math texts open on the kitchen table. I was struggling to do the exercises, even with the answers in the back of the books. That's when Mia appeared on her balcony to give the wrought iron fence a second coat of paint.

She looked as beautiful as the first day I'd seen her there. I watched her for a few minutes, knowing she couldn't see me through the blinds. But something about it didn't feel right. It was one thing to secretly watch Mia when I didn't know her. Now that we going to the movies together on Friday night, it seemed more like spying. So I picked up the math books and headed to the living room, on the opposite side of the apartment.

There I had to deal with the TV and stereo as a distraction. Of course, I wasn't the slightest bit interested in mathematics, which made ignoring those things harder. I knew my seven times table cold from being a football fan—7, 14, 21, 28, 35, 42—the same as six touchdowns and six extra points. But I didn't know a sine from a cosine, and my train of thought kept going off on tangents.

I went to the refrigerator for a snack. That's when I saw Mia had company on the balcony. There were two other girls I recognized as her older sisters and a guy who stood awfully close to Mia.

I knew it was wrong of me, but I kept on watching anyway. The four of them appeared to be having a good time as Mia painted. But every time Mia said something, the guy beside her smiled and laughed harder than everyone else.

Finally, I picked up a phone and called Angelo, hoping he could talk me down from being a spying jealous fool.

"You think they're together?" I asked Angelo, after describing the situation.

"What's the difference? You just got a date with her. You're not *dating* the girl," he said.

"I can't argue with any of that," I said.

"You're going to have to keep your eyes off that back balcony. You're not going to be able to have any kind of a relationship with her if you don't," said Angelo. "For all you know, that's her cousin. Or one of her sister's friends."

That all sounded smart and reasonable, until I hung up the phone. Then I watched the dynamic between those two for another five minutes until I managed to pull myself away.

I didn't get much studying done after that. But I did get out of the house and went for a run to Astoria Park to clear my mind.

By the time I returned, both of my parents were home from work. Mom already had a meat loaf cooking in the oven, which made the temperature of our kitchen almost unbearable. Mom was watching the six o'clock news on TV, and Dad was sitting on the couch beside her, doing the word jumble in the newspaper.

"I'm jumping in a quick shower before dinner," I said.

With the cool water running over me from the showerhead, I felt like all that unfounded jealousy was being washed away. Then I stepped out of the shower and looked myself in the eye in the bathroom mirror.

"You know, you really need to be secure," I told myself.

I toweled off and emerged from the bathroom feeling renewed and in control of my emotions again.

"Dinner!" shouted Mom from the kitchen.

My regular seat at the dinner table faced the window. I took it without so much as glancing up from the plate in front of me. I built a mashed potato fort to hold back the brown gravy, floating the peas and carrots in the moat I made. Then I dug into a wide slab of meat loaf.

About five minutes into the meal, I heard a loud, high-pitched laugh from outside. It was Mia. She was out of her painting clothes and standing alone with that guy on the balcony.

I grabbed my plate of food and bolted.

"Where are you going?" asked Dad.

"The living room," I answered. "It's way too hot to eat in the kitchen."

SELF-REFLECTION: SELF-RELIANCE

Independence and self-reliance are probably the most common traits shared by streetballers. Though in our minds we may picture six (half-court) or ten (full-court) players competing against one another, the truth is that most serious players begin their journey by spending hours alone at a basket, polishing their skills. That takes a good amount of independence. So does walking onto a streetball court, announcing your presence, and staking your claim to play in the next game. Ballers are also very skilled in self-reliance. Whenever they see a hole in their own game—a flaw in their on-court skill set—they usually take it upon themselves to address the problem through practice. And when a shoelace or sneaker breaks during a game, they don't call time-out and run to the nearest Footlocker. Instead, they'll use anything they can lay their hands on at the moment—a rubber band, a piece of tape, or even a plastic bag or athletic sock torn into strips and used as makeshift string—in order to remain on the court.

17

PROBLEM SOLVING

That Wednesday night, the Proving Ground was packed. On Saturday mornings those courts were our oasis, our personal playground. But not on summer nights. Our clique of ballplayers was outnumbered probably ten to one. We were in the minority in a sea of lesser ballers, people on the handball courts, parents with their little ones on the kiddie swings and in the sprinklers, teens with radios hanging out on the benches, older dudes just off work and downing beers, and that small group of dealers by the fountain at the far end of the park.

Despite those numbers, just a few minutes after our first ten players arrived, that tide of lesser ballers parted in our presence. And we stood on the main court ready to choose up a game.

"Are we going to clear the sideline of any potential weapons?" mocked Jumbo.

Though his eyes were cast skyward when he said it, that comment was aimed directly at Pirate.

"Relax. Nobody ever served three-to-five in prison for assault with an ice cooler. You don't know the neighborhood where I grew up. That wasn't a *weapon*. That was a *present* I was trying to give you," retorted Pirate, who slapped hands with several players, cracking up at his own brand of humor. "Sorry, Jumbo. I was out of line for picking something up. You hit me with that big body, so I should have hit you back with mine."

"If you would've hit Jumbo with your scrawny old body, you'd have cracked in two," sniped Gene the Dream, before pointing to me. "Remember how your collarbone snapped when you tried to ram the kid?"

That was the last thing I wanted revisited. I didn't need that ringing in Pirate's ears, perhaps putting a target on my back if he lost his temper later. And I especially didn't need to be in any potential conflict with Pirate while I was carrying that reading class flyer in my back pocket for him.

"Don't remind me. I was just beginning to like that kid," said Pirate. "You don't believe you can whip my ass, do you, Paulie?"

"Who, *me?*" I replied, with just enough bend to my voice to get a laugh but not sound weak.

Then Gene shot out a straight arm into my shoulder, knocking me four feet back and nearly off my feet. That got an even bigger response, with Pirate laughing the hardest.

Hot Rod and Round Mound were the first ones to hit fouls shots. So they chose up the sides. As I could have predicted, Jumbo and Pirate landed on the same squad. That's how it gets arranged when people want to see two players bury a personal beef. If not, the guys choosing make sure they're on opposite teams and guarding each other.

Five minutes into the game, that incident with the ice cooler was almost ancient history.

A guy named Mario was guarding me. He was driving a Wise Potato Chip truck for the summer, making deliveries to groceries and supermarkets. Mario had seen me walking through the streets once and given me a ride to the courts. Only he was steamed as anything when I walked into the park ahead of him to be the tenth player, while he was number eleven and left waiting to play next.

"If I didn't pick you up, I'd be number ten, and you'd be sitting," Mario complained to me.

He was absolutely right. I felt terrible about it. So I never accepted another ride to the courts from anyone. I would rather try to outrun a car that was a few blocks away from the park, hoping it might get stuck behind a red light or two.

Mario was a really good defensive player. He'd chase me all over the court from end to end. What made him an even better defender for the Proving Ground's style of play, though, was that he had no problem grabbing you around the waist and never letting go.

I didn't mind so much, because if I could score on Mario, who usually had a death grip on me, then I could walk into any other park in the city and practically score at will.

That night, I turned to Mario mid-game and said, "You better hope I don't turn up dead in the street later."

"Why's that, Paulie?" he asked.

"Because your fingerprints are going to be all over me," I answered.

Eventually, Monk showed up wearing his street clothes—I guess so he wouldn't be tempted to play or talked into a game.

In between games, Monk came onto the court and said, "I'm leaving for college this weekend. I just wanted to say good-bye to everybody."

The reception he got from the Proving Ground regulars was on the cold side. Only Jumbo, Hot Rod, and I shook his hand.

"So why aren't you playing tonight?" Round Mound questioned Monk. "You'd have a few days to recover from the beating we'd put on you."

"Yo, hump—I mean Monk," said Pirate, "when you try out for that college team, tell the coach that you know an old man who's looking for a scholarship. I'll teach them soft college boys how to play hard."

"I'll let the coach know," said Monk, laughing it off.

I could tell, though, Pirate was only half joking.

Soon the next game began. But we didn't make it until halftime when all the balling suddenly got cut short. That's when three unmarked vans unloaded maybe twenty officers who stormed through the gates and converged on the far end of the park where those dealers had set up their dirty business.

"It's interesting how guys who are into drugs are always looking to get other guys involved, as if they want company when they go under. Me? I was always into basketball." —Nate "The Skate" or "Tiny" Archibald, Basketball Hall of Famer and NBA champion

"We keep thinking that somehow or another if we're going to sell drugs or finance drugs or use drugs that something good is going to happen. Nothing good is ever going to happen concerning drugs. . . . It's that illusion. People keep thinking if they get involved something's going to change. You know what changes? Where you live. You go from that address to a maximum security prison [or] a graveyard." —Richard "Pee Wee" Kirkland, iconic streetball player who served time in prison for running a drug ring

There was a loud stream of applause from us and nearly every-one else there when the cops had those dealers up against the fence, patting them down.

"You're lucky it's just the police," hollered Big Reggie at those dealers. "If you ever sold drugs to my kids, I'd beat you like a tambourine."

Then the cops emptied out the entire yard, before searching eve-ry paper bag beneath every bench.

"Sorry to end your fun, fellas," one officer told us. "This is the way it's going to be tonight."

"No problem," responded Pirate, with a still half-toothless grin. "I'm relieved. When you guys come busting in, I thought you might be after me."

"Why? Are you wanted for something?" asked the officer.

"Only on the basketball court," answered Pirate, slapping hands with Surfer Joe. "If you only knew how we played this game down here, you'd have to put up a police precinct across the street."

Once we hit the sidewalk, everyone was either walking home or headed for their cars. But I still had the flyer in my pocket for Pirate, waiting for the right opportunity to give it to him.

I hung around for five or six minutes, pretending to watch the cops. Finally, Pirate approached his car with no one else within earshot.

"You need a ride somewhere, Paulie," Pirate asked.

"No, I wanted to give you this," I said, producing the flyer. "There are adult reading classes at night at the library on Steinway Street. It's Thursday and Friday nights at seven o'clock."

I'd written at the top of the paper in big letters and numbers "THURSDAY, FRIDAY, 7 O'CLOCK" so he wouldn't have to bother wading through the rest of it.

"So you listen to people when they talk," said Pirate, taking the flyer from my hand and tossing it onto the dashboard of his car. "I appreciate that. Maybe I'll look into it."

I sensed that was all he wanted to say about it.

"That's great. I'll see you Saturday," I said, walking away.

"Did you need a ride?" Pirate called after me.

"Nope, I'm good," I answered, keeping forward momentum.

18

NO RATING

Friday night came, and I didn't tell my parents that I had a date. But by 6:45 they had started to piece the signs together themselves.

"Is there a reason that your hair is actually combed?" Mom asked me.

"Yeah, she must have a name," Dad quickly followed up. "You know there are nose prints on our kitchen window. That would be normal if your mother and I had a dog. But we don't. Just you."

"What is this? One of those TV detective shows?" I said, annoyed at their observation of details.

"You're lucky this isn't one. You'd already be found out," said Mom, an instant before I started down the stairs.

"So you don't want to tell us her name?" Dad called after me.

"No," I answered, reaching for our front doorknob.

"How about where you're going?" asked Mom.

"To a movie," I replied, before I stepped outside.

Then I actually walked the long way to Mia's house, so if my parents were at the kitchen window, they wouldn't see me through the alleyway.

On the way over there, I pushed every thought about that guy on the balcony with her as far out of my mind as possible.

I knocked on Mia's door, and one of her older sisters answered.

"Hi, Paul. I'm Cassie." she said, kissing me on the cheek. "I think this is the first time I ever seen you when you weren't sweaty and carrying a basketball."

Suddenly, Mia was right behind her, looking a little embarrassed by what her sister had said to me.

"Well, if I never put the basketball down, I wouldn't miss it so much," I replied, with a smile.

"See," Mia said to Cassie. "I told you he wouldn't bring that ball to a movie."

It was a four-block walk to the subway, and we talked all the way there.

"So, what are you going to study at school?" I asked.

"Accounting," Mia answered. "I'm really into math and numbers. And I've read those textbooks I saw you with. I know almost every page of them."

"You're *way* ahead of me in math then," I said. "I'm much better with words and ideas."

"Maybe you should major in English," she said. "I read lots of storybooks when I was younger. But now I won't read anything unless it's presenting a problem to solve—one with a concrete answer."

"You know TV and movies are just like storybooks," I said. "Except they're doing the reading for you."

"I don't watch much TV," said Mia. "And I haven't been to the movies in a while."

"Doesn't your little sister watch cartoons and kid shows," I asked.

"Sometimes I have to suffer through that," said Mia, before she added with a widening smile. "And my older sisters like cartoons too."

We got on the train just before the doors closed, and it pulled out of the station almost immediately.

"By the way, have you ever heard of 'Pistol' Pete Maravich?" I asked Mia, with the train rumbling over the tracks beneath us.

"Is he a bank robber?" she replied.

"No, he's a famous basketball player," I said. "Tell Cassie that when Pistol Pete was a teenager, he'd take a basketball to the movies. He'd sit in the aisle seat and dribble all through the flick."

"That's insane," she said. "Did they kick him out of the theater?"

"I'm not sure," I answered. "But tell your sister I never even thought about doing something like that."

Twenty minutes later, we stepped off the subway with the theater just a few blocks away. Two guys walking toward us in the street were mouthing off and looked to be drunk, so I grabbed Mia by the hand and pulled her closer to me.

"Always look like a team," I told her. "Two of them. Two of us. They don't feel like they have an advantage."

We passed those guys without a problem. But I held Mia's hand until we reached our destination.

The movie title on the marquee was in French. Neither of us knew the translation, and the film didn't have a rating. It was a small theater with just one screen, but the place was crowded. We grabbed some popcorn and found two seats together in the back row.

"It must be a good movie, or it wouldn't be on that professor's syllabus," I said.

"Are you going to take that class?" Mia asked me.

"Maybe. I don't register until next week," I answered.

A moment later, the theater lights dimmed, and the movie came on the screen. It opened with a man and woman having wild sex with lots of grunting, gasping, and groaning. They weren't under the covers either. They were totally exposed and going at it hard.

Mia immediately dropped her eyes to the floor.

I was about to say something to her—like "I'm sorry" or "Do you want to leave?"—but before I could, she excused herself.

She disappeared into the bathroom and stayed there for nearly ten minutes.

When Mia came back to our seats, I said, "Listen—"

"It's not a problem," Mia said, interrupting me. "Let's just watch the movie."

"I hate to break the bad news, but it's all in French with English subtitles," I said apologetically. "You okay with reading a movie?"

For some reason Mia insisted on staying. The movie was a total disaster. But at least there wasn't another heavy-duty sex scene.

I spent the entire ride home on the subway trying to get that relaxed feeling back between us. With about four stops on the train to go, she started to almost smile again.

"Maybe the professor teaching that movie class speaks in subtitles," I joked, getting her to laugh out loud.

Walking home, I reached for Mia's hand. Only she pulled it away this time.

"My father's friends are always drinking coffee in these small cafes," she said pleasantly enough. "I don't want them reporting back to him."

I accepted that, thinking about how I'd hid this date from my own parents. But for the first time that night, the guy from the balcony slipped into my thoughts.

When we got to Mia's front door, I kissed her goodnight. And she didn't hesitate at all in kissing me back. Then I walked around the block twice before I went home, trying to figure out if I'd actually had a good time or not.

* * *

The next morning at the Proving Ground, Surfer Joe and Snake chose up sides. I couldn't believe the players that got picked ahead of me. Naturally, Pirate, Jumbo, and J-Train were among the first chosen. But Big Reggie, Hot Rod, Gene the Dream, Mario, and Round Mound—bruisers who'd play defense with a wooden two-by-four in their mitts if they could—were all picked ahead of me. In fact, I was the tenth and final player chosen for the first game.

That was a major blow to my pride. I couldn't remember ever being picked last. I had twice the talent, on both offense and defense, of half the ballers in that yard. So it was easy to see that brute strength and the ability to foul someone hard was being valued above everything else.

What really set me over the edge, though, was that a dude named Antonio couldn't wait to guard me.

"I got Paulie. I'll make sure he doesn't score," Antonio told the guys on his team.

Antonio was probably a decade older than me. I had a ton more footspeed, a half inch in height, and probably ten pounds of muscle on him.

I could understand if Antonio was delusional about his own game. Only his teammates seemingly agreed we'd be a good match. Maybe Angelo, who wasn't there that morning, wanted the weakest player in the park to guard him so he could score. But not me. I was plain insulted.

Just before the start of play, Pirate and Jumbo, who were both on my squad, gave me a wink.

"You know what to do here, Paulie," said Pirate. "Make them pay for this mismatch."

"I can see it in Paulie's eyes," said Jumbo. "He's already on line at the bank to cash this check."

"Next teller, please," I said, in a cold voice.

I blew past Antonio and nailed the first four shots of the game. I watched his defensive confidence dwindle with each bucket made by my hand. Meanwhile, I was becoming more and more supercharged. I made sure Antonio wasn't even close enough to be in my dust. Instead, I'd basically left him in another zip code.

At 4–0, J-Train angrily called time-out.

"We're making a switch right now. You can't guard that boy," J-Train exploded at Antonio. "I didn't wake up early on a Saturday morning to sit on the sideline waiting next."

That speech out of J-Train's mouth hit all the right chords with me.

"You should always play this way—with that chip on your shoulder," Pirate said to me in a low tone.

I wanted to ask Pirate if he'd checked out that reading class at the library. But I was smart enough not to bring it up in public, especially on the court.

I stayed hot shooting the rock that entire morning.

Eventually, J-Train asked me, "You trying to ruin my whole Saturday? I haven't won a game yet."

"I just want to see if I ever get picked last again," I answered.

I was exhausted. Between games, beside one of the benches, I stretched out on the asphalt. I could feel the heated ground beneath me, like I was in some kind of incubator. When I finally got up, my dampened silhouette remained behind, like a sweat-stained snow angel.

A few minutes later, when I chased the ball out of bounds. I saw that my silhouette had almost vanished, evaporating into thin air. That was a lot like the shadow of our original crew—Jumbo, Angelo, Hot Rod, Monk, and me—fading away in the dog days of August.

SELF-REFLECTION: EVOLVING COMMUNITIES

Societies aren't static. Rather, they are dynamic communities—in motion, always changing and evolving. Members of a particular society are arriving and leaving all the time. Streetballers understand this type of flux. The population of streetball colonies in the city's parks is always shifting for various reasons, such as school and work schedules. That's how it was with our original crew. Angelo and Monk already had one foot out the door, hoping to join their college teams and that society of ballers, which undoubtedly would have different goals and mores. Meanwhile, Jumbo, Hot Rod, and I were basically being absorbed into the Proving Ground regulars. Eventually, it morphed from "us" against "them" into a feeling that we were all together. Acceptance of the three of us also meant things were slowly starting to change at the Proving Ground, as we each brought our personal beliefs and attitudes along with us.

19

ROLE MODEL

On Sunday, I met Angelo at the courts beneath the Triborough Bridge. My body was sore and aching all over from balling the previous morning at the Proving Ground. In comparison, Angelo was playing on a fresh pair of legs, having skipped those wearing battles. After five exhausting minutes of going one-on-one against him, I decided to simply play caddie for Angelo, passing him the rock so he could continue to polish his jumper.

"I would have never let that happen at the movies with Mia—be totally ambushed by a wild sex scene," said Angelo, an instant before I delivered a crisp chest pass to him at the top of the key and he drained the shot.

"Really? How would you have known? There was no review of it in the newspaper. I checked," I said, retrieving the rock for him.

"It's simple. I would have seen the movie first by myself. Then there wouldn't have been any surprises," he said, sliding to his next spot, a few steps beyond the left elbow.

"That would have been a crazy amount of trouble," I responded. "More work than fun."

"Yeah, but you only get one chance to make a first impression," he said, asking for the ball with his open hands. "And on a first date, that initial impression is even more important. My prediction is you won't get this girl back to another movie anytime soon. Not unless she picks it."

"I wouldn't ask Mia to another movie," I said. "Maybe a picnic in the park. Something where we could just sit in the sun and talk."

"How'd it go with Pirate and Jumbo? Was it round two?" asked Angelo, missing his first shot of the morning as the rock rattled around the rim and out.

"You're way out of the loop. They both put that nonsense behind them on Wednesday night," I replied.

"Sorry, I got better things to do than stay tuned to Pirate's personal soap opera—*As the Pointed Elbow Swings*," mocked Angelo.

"Pirate was actually pretty calm yesterday," I said.

"Until he blows another mental fuse and goes after somebody," said Angelo.

"Deep down, Pirate's a good guy," I said.

"Sure, he's the type to show up at your funeral crying and carrying flowers. After *he* was the one that killed you," said Angelo, pounding the rock in his left hand. "You think too much of him, Pets. He's not a hero, and he's not a role model. Pirate could become a bad influence on you."

"No way," I said defiantly. "Other than having a passion to ball, I'm nothing like him."

* * *

Late Tuesday afternoon, I was itching to get my body moving. I wanted to put it in motion and keep it that way for a while. So I hustled out my front door. With my first step into the street, without a single thought about stretching, I started running at just a half stride off full speed.

I quickly turned the corner and ran down Mia's block. In my mind, even if she was sitting on her stoop, I was going to stay focused and run right past. The only way I'd stop was if she hollered my name or jumped out in front of me. Forty yards from her house, I decided I wasn't even going to look at her stoop. I was going to keep my eyes focused straight ahead. But just as I hit the adjoining driveway, I heard a voice and glanced off to the side.

It was Mia's little sister, jumping rope on the pavement.

Nice way to stick to a plan, I mocked myself.

When I hit the bottom of the block, I never broke stride. I turned right and saw Snake's sleek Corvette parked on the corner. Revving my own engine a little more, I sailed on past, leaving it in my dust.

To my left stood the massive Con Edison electric plant, with its huge generators and coils that sat in the open yard, sometimes humming in the extreme heat. A block off to my right was a Carvel ice-cream store that Dad had named "Free-vel." That's because during a big blackout one steamy July, when Con Edison went down for something like fourteen hours, all the ice cream in that store was about to melt. So the owner gave out cones and sundaes to everyone for free. To this day, plenty of people in our neighborhood still called it "Free-vel."

"I coined that name," Dad would say, whenever anybody used it in front of him. "I should get a nickel every time it comes out of somebody's mouth."

The Proving Ground came up fast in front of me. There were games going on, even one on the main court. But I could tell by a quick peek that the ball being played there at the moment wasn't worth my time. Especially not in the shadow of staying fresh for tomorrow night.

I sprinted almost another mile up to La Guardia Airport, where the commercial jets come roaring in, maybe two hundred feet overhead. If you're ever standing in their landing path and look up at the right time, those fleet jets will leave you with the feeling that you're going absolutely nowhere.

Across the street from the airport was a row of single-family houses. That's where a neighbor used to take us kids trick-or-treating for Halloween.

"People who own their own homes have money," he'd say, as I piled into the backseat wearing a Captain America mask and carrying a plastic shield with a star in its center. "They give out full-size candy bars. Not those cheap mini ones."

That neighbor was right and had us trek there practically every year.

A half mile later, turning back toward home, I heard the sound of a ball bouncing in a small yard almost hidden behind a freeway underpass. I'd played there maybe once before in my life. The place had never made much of an impression on me. But this time, as I was running by, I saw somebody on the court put down a move that caught my eye.

I came to a stop on the street, breathing hard. Then I saw a second sweet offensive move by that same player. That's when I decided to jog inside.

There were six guys playing half-court, three-on-three, with another body on the sideline waiting for next.

"I've got next with you," I told that lone guy waiting, pointing a finger toward the center of his chest.

He nodded in response.

The scorer on the court who'd caught my eye stood about six foot one, slightly taller than me. He possessed a solid first step to the hoop and a quick release jumper that was consistently finding the bottom of the basket. He was being guarded by a guy probably six foot four, with long arms and a lot of reach. Only that defender wasn't up in his face. The two of them were obviously friends, and the taller guy was just going through the motions, basically getting eaten alive by that scorer.

I wanted to see what that scorer could do against me, against someone who hungered to stop him cold. The more I watched his moves, the more I could see the slight holes in his game. I studied his timing and the angle he raised up with the rock to get it into shooting position.

By the time that game finished, I walked onto the court confident I was about to shut that scorer down. Only I hadn't counted on the fact that we needed another player—one of the losers to complete our three-man squad.

The tall dude who'd been guarding the scorer asked us, "Can I run with you guys?"

My partner told him, "Sure."

I stood right in front of the scorer and handed him the rock.

"I'm not a role model. . . . Just because I dunk a basketball doesn't mean I should raise your kids." —Charles Barkley, Basketball Hall of Famer and TV analyst

"Charles, you can deny being a role model all you want, but I don't think it's your decision to make. We don't choose to be role models, we are chosen. Our only choice is whether to be a good role model or a bad one." —Karl Malone, Basketball Hall of Famer

That's when the tall dude said to me, "What do you think you're doing?"

"I'm guarding your friend here," I told him curtly. "What does it look like I'm doing?"

"I always guard Milo," he said with a lot of attitude.

"Well, not anymore," I responded, looking him dead square in the eye. "This game, he's mine."

"You're not going to be able to stop him," said the tall dude.

"I just watched him take *you* apart piece by piece. You didn't even seem to care," I said. "I can't help but do better."

"Yeah, how about I don't play?" snapped the tall dude.

"Great, don't play," I replied, almost laughing at him. "I could find somebody off the street to play with more passion than you."

Then the tall dude cut in front of me to be in a position to guard his friend. So I lowered my shoulder and shoved him out of the way.

"What's your problem?" the tall dude raged, with Milo holding him back.

"You're the one with the problem," I said. "You've got bad hearing. I already told you, I'm guarding him."

The tall dude might have beaten me into the ground. Somewhere in the back of my mind I heard Angelo's voice. *Pirate could become a bad influence on you.* At that instant, I made the connection between me and Pirate and how I was acting. But I was already into that argument too deep. I wasn't about to back down.

So I just glared at the tall dude, ready for anything.

"It's not worth it," Milo told him. "Let's just play ball."

After exhaling—*huh*—so loud that people in the next county might have heard him, the tall dude stepped aside and groaned, "Okay. Let's see what this guy's got."

That was the moment I felt like I owned them both.

Play started, and I instantly put the clamps on Milo. He couldn't find a good shot to take. My hip was jammed into his and he didn't have any path around me. I had him completely boxed out, so I grabbed nearly every rebound.

That's when something magical happened. Something that could only take place on a basketball court between strangers.

I found the tall dude cutting open to the basket and fed him for an open layup. I did that three more times inside the next few minutes. Suddenly, the tall dude was exchanging high fives with me. Then I delivered the ball to our third player, who scored too.

That game was basically over five points after it began. We won easily, and Milo only scored on a desperation shot near the end, one from almost thirty feet away that I dared him to take. That was alright by me. I understood that left him with at least an ounce of pride.

"Why don't you guys show up at the Proving Ground on Saturday morning," I said, jogging out of the park. "That's where I play. But be prepared."

All the way home, I made a mental list of how Pirate and I were different.

20

B-BALL PARADISE

On Wednesday, for lunch, I went into our fridge. Only the cold cuts bin was completely bare. It was usually filled with spiced ham, bologna, olive loaf, and yellow American cheese. But Mom must have missed her supermarket run.

Then I noticed there was a handwritten note and $6 on the kitchen table. The note read, "Buy yourself something for lunch. Don't go to play ball on an empty stomach. —Love, Mom."

I'd been missing dinner to play Wednesday nights at the Proving Ground. I'd leave the house at around 5 p.m., before my parents got home, and wouldn't get back until almost 8 p.m. Mom always kept dinner warm for me. But most of the time, I was too hyped from playing to eat.

My uncle Eddie ran an Italian grocery store just a few blocks away. So I headed over there.

One time I was in my uncle's store with Beans and another kid named Raffy, who wasn't too bright. I ordered a ham and cheese hero with lettuce and tomato. First, my uncle took out the ham. He sliced it on the stainless steel slicer, carefully rewrapped it, and then put it back into the cold cuts case. Then he did the same with the cheese.

When my uncle, who'd always had a little bit of a temper, was finished making my hero, he turned to Beans and asked, "What do you want?"

"The exact same thing," answered Beans. "Ham and cheese hero with lettuce and tomato."

My uncle nearly went berserk on him.

"Why didn't you tell me that when I had out the ham and cheese," he hollered at Beans. Then my uncle turned to Raffy in a totally irritated tone and asked, "Is that what you want too? Ham and cheese hero with lettuce and tomato?"

Raffy shook his head no.

Five minutes later, after those cold cuts got put back into the case for a second time, Raffy ordered a ham and cheese hero *without* the lettuce and tomato. My uncle Eddie exploded and banished the three of us from his store.

In my mind, Uncle Eddie was like the Pirate of deli meats.

I hadn't been back to the store for a sandwich since. So I figured it might be a good time to finally make amends. But when I looked through the grocery's window, Uncle Eddie was already mobbed by a lunch crowd, as he juggled loaves of bread, industrial-sized jars of mustard and mayo, and a huge carving knife. Then I watched him mouth something tense to one of his impatient customers. That's when I decided a trip to Mickey D's might be the better option for me.

I came out of the Golden Arches carrying a cheeseburger and a Big Mac in a bag. In my other hand, I had a cardboard container of fries, which I always ate while they were still hot. It blew my mind that Mr. Ray Kroc, the guy who owned Mickey D's, also owned the San Diego Padres baseball team. And that the Padres' uniforms were the same color combination of yellow and brown as a Big Mac's secret sauce.

Turning the next corner, I saw Mia and her sisters walking on the other side of the street, headed in my direction. Then Mia crossed over on her own and approached me.

"There's a healthy lunch for you," she said, an instant before she helped herself to one of my fries.

"I'm not worried. I'll burn those calories off playing ball tonight," I said.

I was wearing a polo shirt with a small emblem of a tiger stitched onto the right side, over my chest.

"I like your little tiger," said Mia, touching it with a finger.

To me, that was a signal I should ask her out again.

"Weather's supposed to be cooler for the next week or so. You want to go hangout in Astoria Park one afternoon?" I asked.

"Sure, I'll do that," said Mia.

Then it dawned on me: after all this interaction with Mia, I didn't have her phone number. So I asked for it.

"You don't want to call my house and have my father answer," she said. "I'll call you."

"You know my number?" I asked.

"No, but I know how to look one up," Mia replied, as her sisters called her name to rejoin them. "Oh, when do you register for school?"

"Friday afternoon," I answered, as she crossed back to the other side.

"Mine's on Friday morning," she said, without ever turning around. "Maybe I'll see you."

As Mia left, I was completely satisfied. I figured that all the pressure was off now. All I had to do was sit back and wait for *her* to call *me*.

Then I even congratulated the little tiger on my shirt.

"Good going, *Tigre*," I said, before I licked the salt from the fries off my fingers.

* * *

That night at the Proving Ground turned out to be special. Not because I won every game or because I hit every shot I took. I didn't. It was special because there wasn't any nonsense. It was just streetball at its very best, and nothing else.

Pirate was completely zoned in to his game.

"I had a rough day at work," proclaimed Pirate. "I've been looking forward to playing all afternoon, like it's my salvation. So let's just get it on."

All the games were extremely hard fought. Every one of them went down to the wire, without a single blowout score. A couple of games even went into multiple overtimes, exceeding the usual sixteen-basket winning score. A team needed to win by at least two buckets to claim victory. So some of those intense battles stretched to scores like 20–18 and 19–17.

The games were so good that even players watching from the sideline were glued to the action on the court, cheering sensational moves and mocking turnovers with the game on the line.

At one point, while I was stuck on the sideline waiting for next, I actually started announcing the game, using an empty water bottle as a microphone.

"Gene the Dream gets the ball down low, trying to carve out space. The rock's knocked away by Jumbo. He shuttles it ahead to Hot Rod, who has just Surfer Joe to beat. But he slows it up, waiting for his teammates. Now Reggie sets a pick that a Mack truck couldn't get through. Hot Rod gets free and raises up with the rock. The shot's blocked out of bounds by J-Train. High fives all around. The J-Train came rolling down the track right on time for that defensive stop. While there's a break in the action, let's get a quick word from our sponsors. Ever want to scream in someone's face? Use Listerine like Round Mound. Just because you can be obnoxious, you don't need to have bad breath as well. And Poligrip. Have an upper denture to pop out before a basketball game? Secure it firmly back in your mouth afterward with Poligrip, the preferred denture adhesive of Pirate."

"You could use some of that Listerine yourself," laughed Round Mound. "Maybe Pirate will make it so *you* need dentures too."

"Not tonight," countered Pirate. "I'm on my best behavior. I'm all about ball. That's it. Say whatever you want, Paulie. But remember, you got time to talk because my squad sent you to the sideline. Talk about that for a while. Eat your heart out while the ballers on the court play."

Pirate was absolutely right. I was having a good time announcing the game. But I would have been a hundred times happier to be on the court balling.

I did get back on the court the very next game. My squad even edged out a tight victory over Pirate's team. I scored a few baskets. But I took even more pride in something else. On the winning point, I hit Mario with a pass, an instant before he found Snake running free to the hoop. I understood where the ball had to go to give us the best chance to succeed. So I delivered it there, into Mario's waiting hands. It was an almost invisible assist on my part. But Mario, who'd clearly seen that chain of events unfold, pointed back in my direction to acknowledge me.

Pirate didn't *offer* to drive me home. Instead, he *told* me get into his car. I noticed he had a wooden baseball bat on the floor in front of the backseat. Only I couldn't envision Pirate taking batting practice with it, at least not on a baseball diamond.

On the ride home, Pirate said, "I just wanted to thank you for that paper you gave me. I appreciate it. You didn't have to do that."

"Did you wind up going to the class?" I asked.

"Not yet. I don't just jump into things like that. I've never been comfortable in schools. But I'm thinking about it," said Pirate. "Maybe this week. Thursday and Friday nights at the library on Steinway Street, right?"

"Yes," I said, as we pulled up in front of my house. "Well, if you ever get any homework or practice stuff to read, I can help you with it if you want."

"Thank you, Paulie," said Pirate, making a fist and connecting it to mine. "And listen, this isn't something to talk about with other people. This is private. Between you and me. I've got a reputation."

"Don't worry. I get it," I said, before I shut the car door behind me and headed up my front steps.

That's when I saw Dad's silhouette in our second-floor window.

By the time I opened the door and climbed the stairs, both my parents were waiting for me at the kitchen table. I could tell they wanted to talk.

"So exactly when do you need to be at school?" Mom asked.

"There's something different about playground basketball. There's a freedom, a time to be uninhibited. . . . There are penalties for making mistakes when you play organized ball." —Julius "Dr. J" Erving, Rucker Park legend, Hall of Famer, and NBA champion (shown in photograph at Harlem's Bill Robinson Park in 1975).

"Sports have become very structured. . . . We don't have time to bring that imagination out. It's a really big concern. In practice [coaching my daughter's youth team], at least once a week, the first 20 minutes of practice I have just imagination play." —Kobe Bryant, five-time NBA champion and Rucker Park participant

"I make my schedule on Friday, at registration. But classes don't start for almost another two weeks. Till the Tuesday after Labor Day," I answered.

"Do you know how many days a week you'll have classes?" asked Dad.

"Not yet. I'll know after I register," I said, feeling a little bit like I was being questioned by prosecutors.

"Have you looked enough at this listing of classes?" asked Dad, pointing at the pamphlet, which was resting on top of the math texts I'd taken out of the library. "Do you know all your available choices?"

"Sure, I do," I answered. "What's this all about?"

"This is an important time in your life, starting college," said Mom. "We want to make sure you're focused on school. Not distracted by other things."

"Like playing ball?" I said.

"That's right," answered Dad. "And this girl out the window who goes to the same school."

"Wow. So you really did your homework on that one," I said, walking away from the table and toward my room.

"We're your parents. We should know these things," said Mom.

It wasn't often that I felt like my parents didn't respect my privacy. But for me, that moment had definitely crossed the line.

21

HITTING THE WALL

The next morning, I was still pretty peeved with my parents. So I set my alarm for 7 a.m., about twenty minutes before they both left for work. I popped out of bed and skipped breakfast. Instead, I went right to the kitchen table with a long yellow legal pad and began making lists of possible classes and schedules.

"Your mother and I wanted you to take registration more seriously. But you can eat breakfast first," said Dad, before downing the last of his coffee.

"Do you want me to make you some toast?" asked Mom, clearly trying to appease me.

"I know how to use a toaster," I answered. "I want to finish this first. Then I'll eat and start reviewing some math."

"Well, I'm glad you took our little talk to heart," added Dad.

That unwarranted comment caused Mom to jab Dad in the ribs. I was glad she did. Because that was exactly what I'd wanted to do, especially since that comment about Mia last night.

I was so geared up that after my parents departed, I kept right on working. I found an English class on basic composition and one on Shakespeare plays. I'd seen *Romeo and Juliet* on PBS. That made it a whole lot easier to understand than reading it flat off a page. I figured the odds were good that the station would show a few more Shakespeare plays before the semester ended. There was also a basic class on psychology that caught my eye. I believed if I could deal with streetballers like Pirate, Snake, and Round Mound, then I must possess a lot of natural smarts about what makes some people tick.

When I finished with that list of classes, I put breakfast on hold again, settling for a glass of OJ. I grabbed those math texts and headed toward the living room couch, just for a change of scenery. I didn't even put on the TV or listen to any music. I just went over problem after problem, while still leaning heavily on the answers in the back of the book.

It was a little after 10:30 when the phone rang. Hardly anyone, except maybe Angelo, ever called at that time. So I sprinted into the kitchen to pick it up, thinking it could be Mia.

I got it by the third ring. Only there was nobody on the other end.

Two minutes later, the phone rang again. This time I could hear a voice. But it was totally garbled, and I couldn't make out who it was. So I turned toward the kitchen window and pulled back the curtains. Then I opened the window and stuck my head outside. I figured if it had been Mia calling, she might see me and step onto her balcony.

I hung my head out the window for more than a minute. Only there was nothing in response except a slight breeze.

After staring at the phone for a while, I thought about hitting *69 to find out who'd called. But if my parents ever saw that on our phone bill, I'd have way too much explaining to do. So to clear my mind, I got on my kicks, tucked a ball beneath my arm, and headed out the door for the Proving Ground.

The yard was empty on a weekday morning. That was fine by me. I wasn't looking for a game. I just wanted to relax and shoot the rock for a while. I wanted to revel in the feel of it—the weight and texture—as it rolled off my fingertips. I was playing with an old leather ball only meant to be used indoors. Over the years, the asphalt had put an absolute beating on it, leaving its grips almost totally bald and transforming its once brown color into a faded gray. It wasn't much to look at. But I'd been playing with it for so long, it felt like it belonged in my hands.

After fifteen minutes or so, somebody showed up to slap a handball against one of the concrete walls beyond the fence. They had a radio blasting, and soon enough, I was shooting and dribbling in rhythm to the music.

Eventually, I looked up and noticed Big Reggie standing at the edge of the court watching me.

"No wonder you can run up and down this court all day long without slowing down," said Reggie. "It's probably all you ever do, just like Pirate."

Reggie was sweating up a storm.

"You been playing somewhere?" I asked him.

"Nah, I just ran over the Fifty-Ninth Street Bridge into Manhattan and back," answered Reggie, pointing to the knapsack slung over both shoulders. "I've got forty pounds of metal BBs in this sack. Here, try it."

I put the knapsack on and almost collapsed from its weight. I couldn't even stand up straight in it, never mind run anywhere.

"That's an intense workout," I said.

"It's my day off from riding a jackhammer. I'm not just going to sit around and get lazy," said Reggie, wiping the perspiration from his brow. "I've done some difficult things, Paulie. I played fullback for a while on a college football team. I've had some professional boxing matches, and in the service I was a paratrooper."

"Paratrooper? You jumped out of planes?" I said, somewhat in shock. "I thought you were afraid of heights. That's why you'd never climb up a telephone pole on your job."

"I'm not afraid of heights. I'm afraid of falling off one of those sixty-foot poles without a parachute," replied Reggie, stealing the rock from my hands. "Come on. We're going to play some one-on-one. You're going to be my last workout of the day."

At that moment, I had little interest in competing. But I didn't feel like I could say no to Reggie—a guy maybe fifteen years older than me who'd probably just run ten miles with forty pounds on his back and was willing to keep going.

"All right. Let's do it," I replied.

"Your ball first," said Reggie, who stood in my face at the foul line and shoved the rock into my chest. "Sixteen-point game."

I had no clue how Reggie could win. He had virtually no offense, and I wondered how he was ever going to score.

I feinted to the right, but Reggie didn't bite. Instead, he took a giant step forward and knocked me back nearly five feet. Before I could regain my balance, he closed the gap between us again, with both his arms spread out wide. And for an instant, it felt like the sun had disappeared.

Reggie refused to let me get any separation from him. Every time I raised up with the ball, he'd either rake me across the arms or rip the rock from my hands. I had Reggie stymied on defense too. He couldn't get off a shot without throwing the ball straight up to the clouds.

We'd played several minutes with no score. Then I got the ball in my hands and sprinted for the sideline. I reached there a full step before Reggie, turned, and then heaved the ball at the basket. I heard the *thppp* of the rock slipping through the rim without ever seeing it.

Then Reggie picked me up off the concrete and said, "Good shot, Paulie. That's 1–0, you."

"You sure you want to play to sixteen?" I asked him, already breathing hard.

"That's Proving Ground rules, what we play to down here," he said. "You don't want to shortchange me now that you've got the lead?"

I shook my head and took the rock from Reggie. He looked tired too. So my plan was to sprint right past him. I didn't bother to fake. I just put my head down and exploded to my right. That's when I ran straight into Reggie's massive chest, bounced to the floor, and lost the ball out of bounds.

"This is a stone wall made out of flesh and bone, Paulie," said Reggie, beating his chest like Tarzan. "You don't have enough weight to break through it. Dudes 250 pounds have tried and failed. I thought you'd have better sense."

Reggie's wide smile never left his face. I never once felt threatened by him, just small in comparison. We went at each other tooth and nail for the next twenty minutes. I was ahead 2–0 and near the point of complete exhaustion.

The next time Reggie extended his huge paw to pick me up off the asphalt, I asked, "How about we leave the game right here and continue it another time?"

"That's fine. But just because you're ahead on the score, doesn't mean you win," he emphasized. "This contest is incomplete."

I agreed.

Reggie secured his knapsack full of BBs on his back before he jogged away. Then I walked home and took a long nap.

SELF-REFLECTION: EXPRESSING YOURSELF

An important feature of any society is self-expression, allowing for personal freedom within the context of a group. When most people think about self-expression, disciplines like music, dance, painting, writing, and even fashion design probably come to mind before sports. Streetballers, however, thrive on the concept of self-expression. It's something they live and breathe. Ballers often give birth to moves that are created in the moment, possibly never to be duplicated again and sometimes even surprising their originators. As with any artist, the observer can admire the player's work, applauding from the sideline if a fan or simply nodding in respect if an opponent. In most societies, self-expression is closely associated with valued qualities such as courage, self-assurance, independence, and creativity. In my experience, that aptly describes the characteristics of most streetballers.

22

SEEING DOUBLE

On Friday afternoon, I took the subway into Manhattan to register for classes at school. I had a second polo shirt with a small tiger on the chest. So I wore it special in case I bumped into Mia, who'd mentioned she was registering that morning.

I found the correct building on campus and entered a huge hall with probably three hundred students sitting at tables with worksheets to figure out their schedules.

"Freshman?" somebody asked me, wearing a T-shirt that read "Staff."

I nodded and got directed to the first big table. It had preprinted schedules on it, with three classes already filled out. Then the girl sitting next to me explained that freshmen had less freedom in making a schedule. That we had to take certain prerequisites—like a basic English, math, and science.

"That's okay," I told her. "I don't want anything harder than the basic classes, especially in math."

She smiled at that and said, "Me, too. It was all I could do to pass math in high school."

After working on my schedule for a while, I added to those prerequisites the class on Shakespeare plays and Psychology 101. Then I was able to stack those five classes on Mondays, Wednesday, and Thursdays—leaving me Tuesdays and Fridays off.

I was totally psyched by that.

I turned to the girl next to me and said, "You know there's even a movie class."

"Did you take it," she asked.

"No way," I answered.

"Why? You don't like movies?" she asked.

"I don't like *those* movies," I replied, getting up to hand in my schedule to see if it would be approved.

The dude at the desk said it would take him about ten minutes to check if those classes were still open. So I left the big hall and walked around the first floor to see if I could *accidentally* run into Mia.

I took an extended tour of the entire building, inside and out. But I didn't see Mia anywhere. When I returned to the hall, my schedule was in front of the chair where I'd been seated. It was stamped "Approved" across the top. Then I noticed a phone number handwritten in the margin. The girl who'd been sitting next to me was gone. That number was written in a blue felt-tip pen—the same kind she'd been using.

I laughed to myself, *I know Mia's name, but I don't have her number. Now I've got this girl's number, but I don't know her name.*

* * *

When I arrived home, I immediately checked the answering machine. I didn't want my parents getting to any message from Mia before I did. I walked in and the machine was blinking with a single message.

It was from Angelo, who wanted me to call him back. So I did.

"You want to take a walk to the library on Steinway Street tonight?" Angelo asked me. "The books for my classes are real expensive. I want to see if any of them are on the shelves up there."

So after supper that night, I met Angelo on his corner, and we headed up to the library together.

"I'd be careful ever calling that phone number," said Angelo. "You don't know for sure it belongs to that girl who was sitting next to you. It could be some other girl's number or even a guy's."

I just looked at him sideways.

"Is that what you *really* think?" I asked.

"The point is that you don't know," Angelo answered. "You need to be prepared for anything."

"Forget that," I said. "What books do you need?"

"Two separate ones on business principles," he answered.

"Maybe I could find a book on Shakespeare plays and save some money too," I said.

"Do you need the comedies or tragedies?" he asked.

"I don't know," I responded. "What's the difference between them?"

"Comedies, you love your life," he replied. "Tragedies, you hate it."

That's when we spotted Pirate's car parked a block and a half from the library.

"He could be washing some store window or cleaning one of the offices around here," I said.

"Or he could be taking that reading class tonight," said Angelo. "And if we walk into the library and he's there, he might think we're spying on him."

I could hear Pirate's voice ringing inside my ears. *This isn't something to talk about with other people. This is private. Between you and me.*

He might see me there with Angelo and totally blow his stack.

"Maybe his car's there because he lives around here," said Angelo.

"Think that's possible?" I asked.

"Unless you believe he lives on a pirate ship," quipped Angelo.

The two of us creeped up to the library's window and peeked inside. There was a table of adults in the back and somebody standing near a chalkboard who looked like a teacher with a pointer in her hand. But neither of us spotted Pirate.

"He could be in the bathroom or something," I said.

It was the first time I ever had to watch my back walking into a library.

"Playing in these parks definitely developed my toughness. I always played against guys older than me. Guys tougher than me that beat me up. That never gave me a foul call whenever I called, 'Foul!' It didn't matter what court I went to. I had to prove why I was on that court. Street basketball is who I am. Everything I've become." —Henry "Smush" Parker, Brooklyn native and veteran of six **NBA** teams

"This is crazy, Pets," said Angelo, advancing toward the door. "We're just here for books. How come we have to be the ones scoping the place out?"

"Because we don't want a comedy to become a tragedy," I answered, carefully following behind him.

* * *

At the Proving Ground the next morning, Jumbo, Pirate, Reggie, Surfer Joe, and I dominated as a team. We won the first four games, barely breaking a sweat. Pirate was on fire, smoking basket after basket. And every time the player guarding me tried to double-team Pirate, I'd make him pay by burying an open jumper.

"You can't walk away from Paulie!" screamed Round Mound. "You have to pick your poison against this squad and stick with it."

Whenever we did miss a shot, Jumbo cleaned up the rebound, tapping balls in around the rim. Surfer Joe set constant picks and screens, while Big Reggie caused general mayhem for the other team.

For the fifth game, we played a solid squad of fresh players with big bodies.

A few early breaks went against us. Then we might have gotten a little tired or complacent, because we went to the half trailing by a score of 8–7.

"We need to play harder," said Jumbo. "We can't just turn it on whenever we want. Besides, these guys we're up against are scrappers. The last thing they want is for us to go undefeated. That's their motivation."

"I hear you, Coach," said Pirate in a sarcastic tone.

Then Pirate went out and missed three straight open jumpers to start the second half. I'd never seen him that off on consecutive shots.

On the third one, Pirate even blamed Surfer Joe for putting the wrong spin on the pass to him.

"You're supposed to pass the ball with backspin on it," Pirate snapped. "Not the opposite way."

The other team started to make some ass-lucky buckets. They even made one with my entire hand shielding the shooter's eyes.

"He sank that shot blind," moaned Jumbo. "You might as well be guarding Ray Charles or Stevie Wonder, Paulie."

The other team had us 15–10, just one basket shy of winning.

That's when Pirate drilled a shot from nearly thirty-five feet out. I could see it was good the second it left his hand. So did Pirate, who turned around and trotted back on defense before the rock ever passed through the rim.

Right there, I could feel the momentum shift. Suddenly, we had those guys on the run. Our squad scored the next four baskets, closing the gap to 15–14. Even if you had a crystal ball and could see the future, there was no way you could convince me that we weren't going to win.

We stopped those guys on D and moved the ball down court. We were working the rock from right to left, searching for an open shot to tie the game. Then Surfer Joe mishandled a pass, and the other team picked it up.

A bus driver named Kenny was trying to streak the length of the court with the ball, only Reggie was in hot pursuit. Kenny was a weight-lifting bull and built like a fireplug. He and Reggie running in tandem were like a two-headed battering ram about to do damage to something.

I outsprinted them both up court and stationed myself in front of them. As Kenny got closer, I was about to strip the rock from his grasp when Reggie plowed through us both. Reggie had reached for the ball too, driving Kenny's wrist bone directly into my chin.

The only thing I could see was stars. I popped up off the ground with the world around me spinning in circles.

"You're all right, Paulie," said Reggie, handing me a towel to wipe the blood from a deep gash. "You just need some salve on that cut. But that's for when you get home. Let's take this game."

It was the other team's ball. I was trying to guard my man. But I was seeing double, and I didn't know which one had the rock. Unfortunately, I chose wrong. The one I didn't guard made the winning shot.

Pirate was pissed at me and stormed off the court.

"Damn it, Paulie. You play great defense the entire morning, except for the last point," chirped Pirate.

I had one hand on the fence, holding myself up.

Then Jumbo studied the cut on my chin and said, "I don't know. It looks pretty deep. I'd forget about the salve. You might need stitches to close that."

23

MENDING WOUNDS

When I got home, I hid inside the bathroom for nearly a half hour, running the shower as a diversion for my parents to hear. I examined every aspect of that gash in the mirror, trying to apply enough steady pressure for it to close. Only it wouldn't. Finally, I cleaned it with peroxide, which stung as much as the walloping I'd taken on the court, and strapped a bandage across my chin.

"What happened to you?" asked Dad, as I emerged from the bathroom.

"I just got cut in the game," I answered, heading for my room. "No big deal."

"Let me see it," said Mom, cupping my chin in her hand as I fought back a wince. "Did you clean it? You don't want that to get infected."

"I took care of it. I'm not a kid," I said, with my parents about to go out on their Saturday afternoon shopping run.

"All right. But later when you change the bandage, I want to see it for myself," demanded Mom.

All the time they were gone, I kept pressure on my chin using an ice bag, hoping to reduce any swelling and at least make it look better. Over almost three hours, I exhausted every ice cube in our fridge, without the time to freeze new trays of water. I even went next door to our neighbors, who had an automatic ice maker built into their fridge, and borrowed some.

Right before supper that night, with my chin totally numb from all that ice, I removed the bandage. The cut hadn't closed and a whole section of my chin just flapped down.

"I think I've got a problem here," I told my parents, walking into the kitchen with a flap of skin hanging loose.

"You're absolutely going to need stitches for that," said Dad, rising up from the table and walking me toward the door. "Let's go right now before that hospital emergency room fills up on a Saturday night."

Mom stayed calmer than I would have thought.

"I don't even want to touch it," she said, kissing my forehead and handing me a clean dish towel. "Use this to keep pressure on it all the way there."

On the bus ride to the hospital, Dad complained constantly.

"It's all about those crazies at the park with you," he muttered. "You don't care how rough they play. Well, I do. Not only am I missing dinner—if my insurance doesn't cover this, it's going to mean money out of my pocket. Money I can't afford. We have bills you know, even more with you starting school."

I walked from the last bus stop to the hospital with my head down. Any time I'd been to the ER before, we'd waited there for hours. So I was surprised when the nurse called my name five minutes after we signed in.

The doctor looked at my chin and said, "You're going to need a tetanus shot for this."

"Tetanus shot?" questioned Dad. "That's for when you get cut by rusty metal."

"You don't think I believe he got cut like this playing basketball," said the doctor in a smug tone. "This looks more like a knife cut. The edges are too clean."

I was shocked at that.

"Doc, I got hit by somebody's wrist bone," I said.

That's when Dad rushed to my defense. For all the complaining he'd heaved at me on the bus ride there, Dad did a total 180 and laced into that doctor.

"You might have a medical degree, but I know my son," said Dad, with a spark of fire in his eyes. "He's a ballplayer. He doesn't run with punks in a street gang. He's a ballplayer because I was a ballplayer. I don't want to hear any more about this knife nonsense. Forget the tetanus shot. Just stitch him up."

It took twenty-one stitches to close that cut. And thanks to that doctor and his wild ideas, Dad complained about *him* and praised *me* on that bus ride home.

* * *

Those stitches needed to stay in for at least six days, so I actually started hoping that Mia wouldn't call till then. I didn't need to explain to another person with a normal perspective the kind of all-out streetball wars I'd been taking part in.

I saw my school schedule on top of the dresser in my room. For a while, I looked at that mystery phone number written on it. I tried to visualize the girl who'd been sitting next to me. It was hard because, for the most part, I'd been staring at all that paperwork in front of me. But I remembered her eyes were a lighter shade of brown, and her voice had a touch of gravel to it. In my mind, I was flipping coins as to whether I should call or not. Only I wouldn't even know whom to ask for if somebody else picked up the phone.

Hi, can I talk to the brown-eyed, gravely-voiced girl?

So, ultimately, I decided not to call.

* * *

That dimwit doctor said I couldn't play ball until my stitches came out. That put me on the sideline for Wednesday night at the Proving Ground. It would be the first round of games I missed there all summer.

Before my parents left for work that morning, Mom laid down the law.

"You're not playing tonight. I've cut you a lot of slack this summer over all this basketball. But not tonight," she said, without an inch of wiggle room. "Do I make myself clear?"

"Perfectly," I replied.

"So you'll be here for dinner?" Mom asked.

"I'm not sure yet," I answered.

That got Dad's instant attention; he focused an intense glare in my direction.

"Don't worry. I heard Mom," I said, before he'd turn down those high beams.

I studied the math texts and did push-ups and sit-ups for most of the day, trying to fill my time. Then at around 4:45 p.m., as I started to get real itchy to feel a basketball in my hands, I dialed Angelo.

"You're lucky those maniacs didn't break your jaw. That would be a major hassle to deal with starting school and probably leave you with no chance to make the basketball team there," said Angelo. "You want to do that, right?"

"I guess," I answered. "I just want to play. I don't care if I'm wearing a uniform or not."

"Playing college ball can really help you after graduation," said Angelo. "You can make a lot of connections. People will remember your name when it's time to get a job."

"I can't argue against that," I said.

"So what time are you heading to the courts?" he asked.

"What makes you think I'm going there?" I countered.

"Because you can't help yourself," said Angelo. "You want to be part of that scene. Those guys could exchange basketball for bowling and you still wouldn't miss a day."

Angelo was right. Five minutes after hanging up with him, I was on my way to the Proving Ground.

As soon as I walked into the yard, guys were commenting about my chin.

"I told you we'd rearrange that pretty face of yours," crowed Round Mound, slapping me on the back. "Paulie may have been good-looking the day he first got here, but there was no way he was going to stay like that."

"The game within the game is the game that only the players see. They experience it in relation to one another on the floor at a particular time and in the middle of the action." —Walt "Clyde" Frazier, Basketball Hall of Famer, two-time NBA champion, and seven-time All-NBA Defensive Team member

"Congratulations. You got your badge of honor," said Pirate, an instant before popping out his upper teeth. "I've got a hundred marks like that. It means you've earned your place on the court."

I stood beneath the rim as guys were warming up, passing the ball to them to take practice shots.

"You're not playing, Paulie?" asked Jumbo, sounding surprised.

"My parents won't let me. Not until the stitches come out on Friday," I answered.

"You had to get stitches?" asked Reggie.

"Yeah, that salve didn't work," I answered.

"I'm sorry about that," said Reggie, squeezing my shoulders. "It was unintentional."

"I never thought I'd see the day Paulie could stand up and not ball," said Jumbo.

"I remember when he played with a 102-degree fever and didn't miss a shot," added Hot Rod.

"He's got to listen to his parents," said Pirate. "There's no shame in that. I wish I'd have listened more growing up."

"No Paulie. No Snake tonight," said Round Mound, calling off the absentees.

"Snake's taking the police test," said Pirate. "He'll pass and make a good cop. He's fearless for his size. Better than some of those stupid traffic agents. Right, Paulie?"

"I won't forget that too soon," I replied, as Hot Rod and J-Train began to choose up sides.

Everyone's name was called, except for mine.

Standing on the sideline that night, I remembered everything I loved about streetball. That's because it was all happening right in front of my eyes. There were ball handlers reading the court, making blind passes to players they hadn't seen break open. Bodies boxed each other out, fighting for position beneath the basket, willing to put every ounce of effort into possessing a single rebound. One-handed, off-balance jumpers somehow found the bottom of the rim, going down as smooth as silk, and I was jealous.

My muscles twitched, reacting to nearly every move on the court. And my heart beat harder as the scores tightened up late in the games.

The only thing wrong with that scene was that I wasn't out there.

24

LESSONS LEARNED

On Friday, I had my stitches removed by our family doctor. She looked over my chin and wasn't particularly pleased.

"It's healing fine. But this is just an average to below-average job of suturing," she said, as I arched my chin into the light for her. "It's going to leave a decent-sized scar. I hope you have good memories of that basketball game. They're probably going to be with you for a lifetime."

"I could think of worse things," I said. "So no problems with me playing tomorrow?"

"If you've got the guts to get back out there, you're good to go," she said.

That was all I wanted to hear.

Five minutes after I got home, I heard a car horn outside. *Honk, honk.* From its tone, my ears instantly knew that it was Jumbo in the Brown Betty. So I hustled downstairs.

"What's up? Reading the meters again at Coca-Cola? I could use one of those bottles with too much syrup," I said, reaching the open passenger side window.

"No. Nothing exciting like that. I'm doing almost a dozen apartment buildings in Marine Terrace. You wouldn't be interested. It'll be all I can do not to doze off," said Jumbo. "And all I wanted was to check on how your stitches were doing."

"Got them removed this morning," I reported. "I'm set to ball tomorrow."

"I wish that was me," said Jumbo. "This is Labor Day weekend. We're spending it upstate at a lake with my wife's family. Don't get me wrong. I'll enjoy it. I'll have a blast with my kids. But I'd rather be leaving at 12:30 after the games."

"You couldn't convince your wife to wait?" I asked.

"Even if I could, the traffic at that time would be terrible," replied Jumbo. "You'll have to tame those maniacs without me. I'll probably catch you Wednesday night. Let me go see about these apartment buildings and how many N/A's I can pencil in."

Jumbo started up the Brown Betty. Then the pair pulled away from the curb and were gone.

* * *

I woke up on Saturday morning with an electric buzz in my bones. I couldn't wait to get back on the court and was the first one at the Proving Ground. A half hour later, we had just seven players, waiting for three more to arrive.

"It's always been this way the Saturday before Labor Day. Guys go away for the weekend, and we struggle to make ten players," said Round Mound.

"We can always start off with some three-on-three," said Hot Rod.

"Wait a little while longer," said Pirate. "I got a guy from work, in one of the offices I clean. He thinks he can play. He's coming down with two friends. That'll make ten for us."

"So the guy thinks he can play. Did you tell him how we roll at this yard?" asked Surfer Joe.

"I told him, 'You and your friends are welcome to come. But we don't want you calling fouls. Or just stay the hell home,'" answered Pirate.

Over the next fifteen minutes, those three new players did show up. The games began, and everything was going along fine until one of them barely got tapped on the wrist and called, "Foul!"

Pirate dropped his head in frustration and warned, "Don't do that. You're going to get my blood boiling."

But Surfer Joe, the one who tapped the guy, exploded, "Do you want to see what we can really do? Wait till next time. I'll give you a reason to call foul. Then you'll see the difference between getting hammered and brushed!"

Two plays later, I grabbed a rebound, and Surfer Joe, who was still angry at that guy, clubbed me over the head with a forearm. As a result, the ball went out of bounds off my hands.

"That's our ball," said Surfer Joe.

"What are you talking about?" I hollered at him. "You hit me in the head."

"That's the point—I hit *you*. Not the *ball*. And it's off your hands," raged Surfer Joe. "Maybe you need to find another park. Ask where these other guys play. You can go there and call foul."

I was pissed and ready to make a stand.

"You're not getting the ball. No way," I said.

"Keep it up, Paulie. I'll hit you again," said Surfer Joe.

I'd had enough of being insulted. I stood directly in front of Surfer Joe and picked up my hands in a boxing stance.

"Go ahead. Hit me now," I challenged him.

"I wouldn't waste my time fighting you. You're less than nothing," he said.

I absolutely lost my mind. I'm not proud of it. But Surfer Joe wouldn't show me the respect to fight, so I spit in his direction. Only that spit from my mouth flew farther than I'd figured, landing right on his bare chest.

Surfer Joe charged me, and I punched him squarely in the jaw.

"Nobody spits on my friend," screamed Pirate, who charged me too, from directly behind Surfer Joe.

Suddenly, I was fighting them both, firing punches blindly.

Everyone else on the court rushed toward us, trying to break up the fight. Then that whole crowd of bodies tumbled forward toward the ground, with me winding up at the bottom of the pile.

Like Bugs Bunny in some cartoon wrestling match, I wiggled out from the bottom, as the rest of them kept on brawling without me. I walked to the benches and grabbed my extra T-shirt to wipe the sweat from my face.

They finally noticed I was gone. Pirate probably thought I was headed home.

"Hey, don't leave. We won't have a game with only nine," screamed Pirate.

"Better not go, you loser," Surfer Joe's voice followed.

That was all I had to hear. If walking out of the yard was going to wound those two the deepest, that's exactly what I was going to do. In a sense, I'd be punishing myself too. But I was over-the-top angry and couldn't play anymore.

I could hear them cursing me from behind, as I walked right out the gate.

* * *

I came through the front door more than an hour and a half before my parents ever expected me. They understood right away that something had happened.

Dad asked, "You want to tell me about it?"

"Nope," I replied, before marching into the bathroom for a long shower.

I turned the faucet marked "hot" up full blast. The entire bathroom filled up with steam, and I kept spitting water from my mouth at the seahorses decorating an ocean-blue shower curtain.

Eventually, Mom left to go shopping. Only Dad stayed home.

After showering, I settled in my room, which was a total mess, with shorts and shirts draped everywhere. I began sorting my summer clothes and school clothes into two different piles on my bed, with a third pile for everything headed into the laundry hamper. Maybe twenty minutes into that massive job, there was a knock at my door.

"Come in," I said, still aggravated as anything.

"Well, at least you're all in one piece this week," said Dad. "You've had a chance to cool down. I want to hear about it now."

"A guy hit me over the head, then wouldn't fight me. So I spit on him and then threw punches with him and somebody else," I said, quickly in a flood of emotions.

"Wait. Wait. Back up," said Dad. "You spit on somebody?"

"I didn't mean to. I meant to spit *at* him," I said. "But first he—"

Dad interrupted and said, "There's no excuse for that. Did you apologize?"

"No, because—"

"There is no *because*," emphasized Dad. "If you don't apologize, you're never going to set things right between the two of you. You might as well never play at that park again. Now think about that."

Then Dad left me alone to stew in my anger and consider what he'd said.

* * *

More than two hours later, I left my room and walked out of the house. I started marching toward Steinway Street. There was a concrete park with a pair of hoops and playground equipment on the opposite side of the block, behind a big public parking lot. I knew that Surfer Joe lived in an apartment building directly across from that yard.

I didn't know his apartment number, what floor he was on, or even his last name to ring a bell. And I didn't know if we'd be exchanging punches again the moment he saw me. But I was headed there anyway, with Dad's words as my motivation.

When I reached his corner, I saw Surfer Joe inside the park, sitting on top of a bench. He was sipping a beer, watching a half-court game being played at one of the hoops there. And sitting right next to him on top of that bench was Pirate.

"You here to spit on me again?" asked Surfer Joe, as I walked into the park.

"I was disappointed in you today, Paulie," added Pirate.

I swallowed hard and said, "I came to apologize."

"I'm listening," said Surfer Joe. "Make it good."

"I was wrong. I should have never done that," I said.

"That it. You done?" asked Surfer Joe, getting off the bench and standing right in front of me. "For the last couple of hours, I've been thinking about nothing but fighting you."

Then I saw his shoulder move and I braced myself for anything.

Surfer Joe stuck out his hand and said, "This was partly my fault, so I'm going to accept your apology. But don't you ever spit at me again."

"I won't. I was wrong," I said, shaking his hand. "My Dad explained that to me."

"See, I told you this kid had some class," said Pirate, punching me lightly in the stomach and getting me to flinch. "You guys want to play three-on-three against the winners here?"

"That's all right," I said. "I've had enough for today."

SELF-REFLECTION: EARNING A REPUTATION

Every society has its subsects populated by those who see things differently from the norm. The Proving Ground was such a place, a complete outlier among basketball yards, where the normal attitudes didn't seem to apply—often resembling the Roman Colosseum for its brutally physical style of play. Many visiting ballers would last a single morning there before vowing never to return. Besides the regulars' distaste for anyone ever calling foul, the normal symbols of status were disdained. If you walked through the Proving Ground's gates wearing expensive and flashy kicks, a high school or college uniform, or even a replica NBA jersey with your favorite player's name stitched across the back, the regulars would focus on making you prove you were worthy of such symbols. And if you ever showed up wearing a colorful headband or wristbands, in the minds of the regulars, you'd better play hard enough to sweat up a storm, warranting their usage. In short, nothing is ever given to you. A streetball reputation, and all it may bring to your life—both today and tomorrow—is something you have to earn. You simply can't purchase it in advance.

25

THE COURT LESS TRAVELED

On Tuesday morning, I attended my first class at school. It was Psychology 101. The professor spoke with a thick European accent. To understand him, I had to replay every word out of his mouth inside my mind. Only at a much slower speed. It was like attending the class twice in a single sitting.

"We will study many different kinds of thought processes and personalities," the professor lectured. "Some of them you will be familiar with. Others not. Some you'll recognize as belonging to your family and friends. A few you may recognize as your own."

A student asked, "Will there be a final exam or a term paper?"

"Both," answered the professor. "The term paper is normally on an alternative society. One with different mores and goals."

Right away, I thought of the Proving Ground.

"How many creative writers do we have in the class? Musicians? Artists? Actors? Athletes?" he asked the students.

By the end of that list, almost everybody had their hand in the air, including me.

The professor said, "Look around the room at each other. Believe it or not, you all share a lot in common. Similar motivations. Rewards and disappointments. And the few of you who don't have your hands raised, it's possible you haven't looked deep enough inside yourselves yet."

I was taking notes, writing furiously to keep up. And I didn't stop until the class ended.

Fifteen minutes later and one floor below, I was searching for my English classroom. Up ahead in the distance, I spotted Mia. She was standing still with her back to me. Then a guy, who'd been drinking water at a fountain, grabbed her hand and the two of them walked down the corridor together.

It was that same guy from her balcony.

They were leaning into one another with every step forward. Then they turned into a classroom.

As I passed that same door, I glanced inside. They were sitting side by side in the first row, laughing and looking into each other's eyes. Up on the board, a dozen or so complicated math problems awaited them.

But I had just solved mine.

I wasn't mad at Mia at all. I was actually relieved.

Then I went off searching for my English class, pondering that mystery phone number, which I already knew by heart.

* * *

The next day, after my last class on Wednesday afternoon, I headed over to an armory a handful of blocks from the school, which didn't have a gym of its own. The sign posted outside the physical education office had read, "Opening Basketball Tryouts. Bring Your Game!"

I'd been to that armory before as a senior in high school. I'd competed in a one-mile race there, running laps around an oval laid out with cones during indoor track season. I walked through the main door and passed several olive green army Jeeps parked inside. There was even a soldier there in fatigues. But I followed the sounds of the bouncing basketballs to where they'd erected a court with baskets and backboards on wheels.

I looked over the crowd of players and understood why it had been billed as "opening" tryouts. The talent on the court didn't appear overwhelming, and I knew instantly that the players from last year's squad probably weren't going to be involved.

A couple of players, though, were wearing their high school uniforms, undoubtedly freshman like myself. They were wearing those uniforms to make a statement to the coaching staff.

Maybe I should have worn my hand lettered Those Five Guys jersey, I thought to myself.

The thing about tryouts is that everybody is there for himself. Only someone looking to impress the coach as a pure point guard will pass the rock to you. Everyone else on the court is basically interested in creating his own shot and scoring.

My best chance to impress the coach was to play defense and rebound. To totally shut down one of those guys in a high school uniform.

Thirty-five players were there, so the coach broke us up into seven teams of five. When my grouping was called onto the court, the other squad had a uniformed dude who was probably six foot three.

My eyes lit up as I walked right over to him.

An instant later, the coach called the guy over for a quick chat. Since he was my man on defense, and I wasn't about to let him out of my sights, I walked over with him.

Dr. J at Harlem's famed Rucker Park. *YouTube.*

"Remember what we talked about, Damon," said Coach. "Play with your back to the basket. I want to see you use a drop-step to get your shot off."

For me, hearing that information was like playing poker against somebody and getting to see their cards in advance. Besides, if the coach was watching that guy, that meant he'd be watching me too.

We had the ball on offense first and turned it over coming to half-court. I immediately sprinted back on defense, as a wave of their players came at me three-on-one. I forced the guy with the rock into a bad shot. But that dude Damon grabbed the rebound and slammed home an uncontested dunk.

There were a few *oohs* and *ahs* from the crowd.

Now I was doubly determined to prove to everyone that I could put Damon inside my pocket and walk away with him.

On offense, I set picks and passed the ball. I even scored our first basket after I fought my way to the rim and tapped in a loose rebound with my left hand.

Damon wanted to post me down low. He had three inches and probably thirty-five pounds on me. I ran the length of the court with him, nearly face-to-face. He smirked, as if he was preparing to swat me away like an annoying fly. When we reached the top of our circle, I drove my hips into his and made him fight for every inch of ground after that. He was stronger. But I had all the leverage and positively stonewalled him fifteen feet from the hoop.

On another trip, Damon received the pass, maybe twelve feet out, with his back to me. I waited for that drop-step the coach had asked for. It arrived right on cue. I faded back with it, like we were dancing a waltz together. Then when Damon, a right-handed player, tried to spin right, I was already there waiting for him. With no-where left to turn, he passed the rock away.

Finally, Damon tried to bull-rush me. Only I had a hand on his waist and could feel that explosion of power coming in his legs. So I stepped slightly off to the side as he pushed through thin air. Then I slid a leg between his two, taking the superior angle. He didn't have the math in his stance to stop me from coming forward, and I shoved him six feet in the opposite direction.

That was the type of algebra I knew.

Then Damon flew back at me. We were in a chest-to-chest stand-off when the coach blew his whistle.

"Next group of ten on the floor," said Coach, carefully watching the interplay between Damon and me.

I walked off the court three feet from Damon, never taking my eyes off him.

Within earshot of the coach, Damon turned to me in anger and asked, "You got some kind of problem with me?"

"No, I've got nothing but respect for you," I replied. "That's why I played you so damn hard."

But as big as Damon stood, I could feel him firmly inside my pocket.

My group didn't get called back onto the court. I didn't know exactly how to interpret that. But an hour later, I was one of the eight players the coach asked to remain behind, after he thanked and dismissed the rest.

Damon was among the eight too.

Coach pulled us together in a tight circle and said, "Two players graduated from last year's squad. That's all the room I have—two spots. Those two new players are likely to never get into a game. At least, not this season. Now I also have a need for several practice dummies. Players to stand around and give the team something to look at. To scheme against. Any questions so far?"

"What's the practice schedule look like?" Damon asked.

"Saturdays, 8 a.m. till whenever. Mondays, Wednesdays, and Thursdays, from 4 p.m. till about 7:30 or so," answered Coach. "No in-and-outers. You must be there every practice or you're gone."

That would stop me cold from playing at the Proving Ground. Even through the winter, when the regulars had told me they were going to get the local junior high gym and still play every Saturday and Wednesday.

"You have to want this bad to make it. If you want to be part of *our* team. *Our* family. There has to be nothing you want more, except maybe an education. Obviously you need to pass your classes to play," said Coach. "But if there's something else on your mind, someplace else you'd rather be, don't waste my time and yours. Be truthful to yourself."

That's when I realized, I already had a basketball family of my own. It may have been a dysfunctional one, coexisting in a house where the walls and foundation got rattled constantly. But it was a family nonetheless.

I didn't want to insult that coach by walking out before he'd finished speaking. But in my mind and in my heart, I wasn't about to walk away from being a streetballer, especially to sit on the bench or be one of his team's *dummies*. I might still have been standing in front of him, but in reality I was already gone. There wasn't even a shred of doubt for me.

A few minutes later, an assistant handed out contact forms to write our names, phone numbers, and addresses. While everyone else was filling out that paper, I changed my clothes and eyed a clock on the wall. It was almost 5:15. I still had an outside chance of making the last Wednesday night game at the Proving Ground.

Just before I walked out of the armory, I balled up that contact form and sank it into an open trash can.

"Swish," I said to myself in a low voice.

All the way back to Queens, the subway was super slow, coming to a complete stop between several stations for nearly ten minutes at a time. Those delays ended my chances of making it to ball.

"Passengers, we apologize for any inconvenience," announced the conductor over a loudspeaker. "There are major signal troubles ahead. I'm afraid it's going to stay this way for a while."

I decided to get off at the Broadway station and walk home the three extra stops from there, probably about a mile. I came down the stairs from the elevated platform with a crowd of others. I'd gone almost two blocks when I spotted five junior high–aged kids on a basketball court beside a small school.

One of those kids was looking longingly down the street, waiting for another player, any player, to arrive.

"Guys, you looking to make three-on-three?" I asked, entering the yard and putting down my books. "I'm that player. Come on. Let's do this thing."

"Even when I'm old and gray, I won't be able to play it, but I'll still love the game." —Michael Jordan

AFTERWORD

Streetball is a society unto itself. Its elements have helped to define a much wider culture, making significant contributions through fashion, film, literature, language, music, and other forms of entertainment and commerce. There is a simple three-word expression that sums it up best: "Ball is life." For there are people throughout the world who have never walked into a ball yard, yet still are familiar with the influences of the game. Let's take a look at streetball's far-reaching impact, without forgetting to recognize the originators of it all—the ballers.

ICONIC KICKS

Chuck Taylors—Chuck Taylor sneakers go by another name, Converse All Stars. Often, they're simply called Chucks or Cons. That's because back in the early 1920s, an American semipro basketball player named Chuck Taylor asked Converse to redesign their basketball shoe to give it more support, better flexibility, and a looser fit to avoid blisters on his feet. The design engineered by Converse was so good that the shoe remains virtually unchanged today— known for its white toe cap, brown rubber sole, and stitched cotton canvas upper portion. By the 1960s, the company had captured the vast majority of the basketball shoe market. Its popularity declined in the 1970s, however, with other companies such as Nike, Adidas, and Puma competing by employing modern-day players to create signature shoes.

Puma Clydes—Perhaps the perfect pairing of a legendary baller and a shoe company came when Puma created a sneaker for New York Knick Walt "Clyde" Frazier. The model was originally released in 1970–1971, a season after Frazier had won the NBA Championship. In addition to his sublime on-court skills, Frazier was known for his stylish clothing. He earned the nickname Clyde, which was inspired by the film *Bonnie and Clyde* about a pair of well-dressed bank robbers. The low-top sneakers, in leather or suede, were known more for their sharp look than for their performance on the blacktop. They also became the favored shoe of many old-school hip-hop artists and the B-Boy (breakdancing) culture. An earlier model of the shoe was held by US Olympian Tommie Smith during his protest against racial inequality during the medal ceremony at the 1968 Summer Olympics in Mexico City.

Air Jordans—In 1984, Nike produced a basketball shoe especially for the Chicago Bulls' rookie sensation Michael Jordan. Later that year, the shoe was made available to the public. Over the next several years, the shoes took flight right beside the storied career of MJ. Filmmaker Spike Lee, playing his Mars Blackmon character, appeared in several Nike commercials with Jordan, inquiring about his on-court talents and theorizing, "It's gotta be the shoes." For a short time, Commissioner David Stern outlawed the original model, Air Jordans I, which had a black-and-red color scheme, from NBA games for not having enough white on them. That seemed to make the public desire them even more. There are currently over thirty different models of the shoe.

Reebok Pump—Released in 1989, the Reebok Pump was the first basketball shoe to contain an internal mechanism (air pump) to produce a customized fit. Two-time slam-dunk champion Dominique "The Human Highlight Film" Wilkins was the original face of the shoe. Then in 1991, while competing in the NBA Slam Dunk Contest, Dee Brown inflated his Reebok Pumps in front of a huge

Air Jordan shoe. *stockelements / iStock Editorial via Getty Images.*

national audience before executing the winning no-look dunk. The next year, Reebok came out with the Dee Brown pump shoe, its tag line "Pump Up & Air Out."

COMMERCIALS

The Nike Freestyle commercial's extended cut, which lasts a little over two and a half minutes, has the feeling of a choreographed ballet. It features a mix of pros and streetballers—men and women—displaying their best freestyle ball-handling techniques (no court, no basket, no competition—just ballers and a rock) as they move in rhythm to the music of "Planet Rock" by electro/funk hip-hop ensemble Soulsonic Force. The commercial dropped in 2001 during the NBA All-Star break, inspiring legions of ballers to practice those same moves in the park. Several months later, the ad was spoofed in *Scary Movie 2* (2001), increasing its profile and longevity.

McDonald's has put together several incredible commercials using ballers. It began in 1993 with "The Showdown." Larry Bird, standing on an empty gym court, spied Michael Jordan about to eat a Big Mac on the sideline. "I'll play you for it," said Bird. "You and me, for my Big Mac?" inquired MJ. "First one to miss watches the winner eat," responded Bird. What ensued was a fantasy-like game of HORSE, played only to the letter *H*. They keep matching each other's shots—one more difficult than the next, until the pair are both standing outside the gym ready to shoot the rock through an open window and have it ricochet into the hoop—*nothing but net*. The commercial became an instant classic, spawning later versions, which included Charles Barkley. The original ad was redone in 2010 with LeBron James and Dwight Howard playing for LeBron's Big Mac.

In 2012, when NBA star Kyrie Irving aged some forty years through several hours in a makeup artist's chair, the Pepsi Max/ Uncle Drew ad campaign was born. It began as a five-minute online video before going viral and reaching TV in thirty-second spots, eventually culminating in a movie, *Uncle Drew* (2018). Irving, disguised as elderly Uncle Drew, enters a packed Bloomfield, New Jersey, streetball yard one evening in the company of his nephew. Uncle Drew takes the place of an injured player. After a shaky start and a few bad misses to sow the seeds of doubt, Uncle Drew kicks it into high gear and simply dominates his younger opponents to the delight of the crowd. "Don't reach [for the rock], Youngblood," Uncle Drew taunts a would-be defender, displaying a deft dribble before blowing past to the rim.

VIDEO GAMES

NBA Street takes the avatars of recognized pros from the bright lights of the arena and brings them to ball yards around the country. They compete playing three-on-three. The winning score is the traditional outdoor mark of twenty-one points. Players can leap to the sky, and goaltending (interfering with the ball on its downward path to the rim) is actually allowed. Flashy plays enable you to get a Gamebreaker, which can not only add to your points but subtract from the opponent's score. Contests can be staged in hardcore yards such as South Beach, Venice Beach, Route 66 in northern Arizona, Chicago's The Loop, DC's The Paint, and New York City's Rucker Park and The Cages at West Fourth Street. NBA Playgrounds adds a different dimension for gamers by allowing great players of the past, such as Wilt Chamberlain and Magic Johnson, to compete against modern-day pros in ball yard settings.

Street Hoops features real-life streetballers such as Half-man/Half-amazing, Hot Sauce, and AO. Gamers can also create and name their own streetball heroes with whom to compete. There are three different modes of play: World Tournament (you're on the road), Lord of the Court (defending your home court), and Pick-Up Game (where the winning avatars earn crisp C-notes as if they'd wagered on the outcome). These characters can even talk trash and throw elbows at one another. 3on3 Freestyle, with an avatar of ball-handling wizard Grayson "The Professor" Boucher, features its own cast of characters with particular core skills, including several female streetballers throwing down hard against the boys.

THE BALLERS: FROM OLD SCHOOL TO NEW SCHOOL

The legendary leaping ability of Earl "The Goat" Manigault has inspired many sensational stories, including one version where the six-foot-one baller would grab a dollar bill from the top of the backboard and leave four quarters in its place. His signature move was the double-dunk, jamming the same basketball twice, without hanging on the rim, in a single jump. Kareem Abdul-Jabbar recognized Manigault, who never played in the pros, as the most talented player he'd ever competed against. "At the time there weren't a whole lot of people who could do things with the basketball that

Earl Manigault could do. He was so agile, so quick. He used to make so many innovative moves to the hoop. Basketball was his total means of expression," said Abdul-Jabbar. The nickname "The Goat" probably arose from the early mispronunciation of his name, *Mani-goat* instead of *Mani-gault*. But fittingly, his streetball tag is an acronym for "the Greatest of All Time." Sadly, Manigault suffered from a heroin addiction, seriously harming his health and causing him to spend several years incarcerated.

In the late 1960s, shooting guard Richard "Pee Wee" Kirkland was a dominant force at Rucker Park. *Sports Illustrated* referred to him as the "fastest man in college basketball." He was even drafted by the Chicago Bulls in 1969. But Kirkland, who was making more money than most pro athletes by financing a drug ring on the streets of New York, passed on a possible career in the NBA. Just a few years later, Kirkland was sentenced to a decade behind bars in a federal penitentiary. Upon his release, the iconic baller earned a master's degree in human services and, along with help from Nike, created "School of Skillz," a program that teaches youngsters the fundamentals of both life and basketball. "This is how you play basketball, a game I always won, and this is how you deal with life, a game I once lost," said Kirkland. "Everything is timing. Thirty years ago, I was part of the problem. Thirty years later, I'm part of the solution." Kirkland and his journey have been mentioned in the lyrics of songs by Terror Squad, Ja Rule, and Future.

Joe "The Destroyer" Hammond didn't play in a single high school or college game. But this legendary playground scorer, known for his deadly bank shot and high-rising dunks, made such an impression on pros playing in NYC's summer leagues that the Los Angeles Lakers selected him in the NBA's 1971 Hardship Draft. He had a tryout playing one-on-one against then Lakers guard Pat Riley (a session reported to be ultra-physical on the part of Riley, who probably didn't appreciate a park player who could conceivably make the team and steal some of his minutes). Hammond turned down an offer from the Lakers because he was making more money in NYC's gambling dens and drug trade. He later declined a contract from the ABA's New Jersey Nets as well. Like other streetball icons of his era, Hammond eventually did federal time on a drug charge, falling victim to the negative side of street life.

Streetball's bridge between old school and new school can be seen in the rise of the dynamic point guard Rafer "Skip to My Lou" Alston, whose star eventually shone brightly in the NBA. This park legend had his early ball-handling sessions videotaped (they can be found on YouTube), helping to inspire the future AND1 Mixtape Tours. Alston earned his nickname through a highly stylized hesitation skipping motion with his legs and feet, while still controlling the dribble, often leaving opposing defenders off balance and out of sync. In 2004, as a member of the Miami Heat, Alston, playing in the backcourt beside rookie Dwayne Wade, helped guide his team to the NBA Eastern Conference semifinals, while averaging over ten points and four assists per game. "To make it to the NBA was always my dream," said Alston. "[But] my style of game, my nickname and my claim to fame would be discovered playing the streetball game."

The producers of the AND1 Mixtape Tour began by going city to city, looking for emerging streetball stars to form a traveling squad.

Stock graphic illustration. *Matrosow / iStock Editorial via Getty Images.*

However, what they found in Philip "Hot Sauce" Champion was something much more. An electrifying talent who could bring fans to their feet in anticipation of his signature collection of "killer" crossover dribbles—the Boomerang, Hypnotizer, Hurricane, and Flintstone Shuffle—Champion truly enjoyed embarrassing opponents. He was a star whose must-see talents mesmerized on ESPN's *Streetball* series and YouTube. "There's more talent than just in New York City," said Hot Sauce, originally from Jacksonville, Florida. "When they came to Atlanta, my name was just a buzz around Atlanta as far as doing the moves, crossing people over. . . . They were looking for hot handles, flair and people who could pass." Champion appeared with the AND1 Mixtape Tour from 2000 to 2004 and 2006 to 2008. He also played the character Jewelz in the 2006 streetball genre film *Crossover*.

Oregon native Grayson "The Professor" Boucher is a ball-handling phenomenon. At approximately five foot ten and weighing 155 pounds, Boucher is the everyman of streetball, making us believe that if he can succeed at such a high level, then maybe so can we. Of course, The Professor has put in an extraordinary amount of time and hard work to maximize his scintillating skills with the rock. "My whole upbringing there was a tug-and-pull with my coaches," said Boucher, who played at Chemeketa Community College in Salem, Oregon, before earning his spot in an open tryout with the AND1 Mixtape Tour. "They didn't like me going outside the system. . . . I never really got that green light to express myself on the court until the AND1 Mix Tape Tour [from 2003 to 2011]." The Professor has become a strong presence on social media and YouTube, ultimately hiring his own production team to document his streetball career, even while disguised in a Spiderman costume and using his legendary handle to defy unsuspecting challengers.

LEGENDARY WOMEN

Sheryl Swoopes and Nancy "Lady Magic" Lieberman both had to overcome huge obstacles at home before they hit the park to hone their future Hall of Fame skills—namely, their mothers. Swoopes's mom believed the game was too rough for girls, and Lieberman's mom actually punctured her daughter's basketballs with a screwdriver to stop her from constantly dribbling indoors during a bitterly cold Brooklyn winter. But both mothers, eventually recognizing their daughters' passion for the game, became supportive. "For all the girls, if you want to play, play," said Swoopes, the three-time Olympic gold medalist who first hit the blacktop in her native Brownfield, Texas. "I've been playing since I was seven [with my brothers]. When I first started, they wouldn't pass me the basketball. They would [only] pick me because they had nine players and needed a tenth to make five-on-five. But I took a lot of pride in proving those people wrong, including my mom." And Lieberman's mother was so proud of her daughter's accomplishments, there was no one, no matter how famous, to whom she wouldn't brag. "So my mother, this little Jewish lady from New York, goes up to [Muhammad] Ali, and tells him that her daughter is the greatest of all time," said Lieberman, who grew up playing in pick-up games against boys. "Ali just looks at her and says, 'Lady, there's only one greatest of all time, and that's me.'"

As kids, Cheryl Miller and her brother Reggie—the first pair of siblings to become Hall of Famers—used to hustle streetball games for money while growing up in Riverside, California. Their ultimate prize in those days? Taking their winnings to Mickey D's to buy Happy Meals. "Basketball taught me to be a respectful person, [and] how to select friends," said Miller, an Olympic gold medalist and two-time NCAA champion.

In 1980, Ann Meyers Drysdale signed a $50,000 no-cut contract with the NBA's Indiana Pacers to compete against men. And though she didn't make the final squad that season, it was a substantial milestone for women athletes. "I think the guys were more nervous than I was. Here was a woman competing against them to play in the NBA," said Meyers Drysdale, the first woman to receive a full athletic scholarship at UCLA. "I was involved in a lot of firsts in my life. Making an NBA team didn't turn out to be one of them." That same year, Carol "Blaze" Blazejowski signed a three-year $150,000 contract with the New Jersey Gems of the brand-new Women's Pro Basketball League. The league folded after its initial season, and Blazejowski claims she never collected a dime for her efforts. But she was certainly never cheated by the experience. "It's passion about what you want to do," said Blazejowski, a New Jersey native and three-time Collegiate All-American, who is included as a hidden player in the NBA Jam Tournament Edition video game. "Passion for me was basketball. . . . Everything about the game was part of my life. . . . Chase your passion, not the money."

BALL YARDS

Holcombe Rucker was a playground director in Harlem over the course of three decades. Through sheer will he started a humble streetball tournament, which began with oak-tag schedules tied to trees. Today that tournament, known as the Entertainer's Basketball Classic, is held in the park that bears his name—Rucker Park—arguably the most famous streetball yard in the world. It is hallowed ground for streetballers, a place where pros like Wilt Chamberlain and Julius Erving faced off against legends like Joe "The Destroyer" Hammond and Pee Wee Kirkland. And it's where a team featuring a trio of New York Knicks immortals, including Walt "Clyde" Frazier, Willis Reed, and Bill Bradley, lost to an amateur squad from a local bar called Sweet & Sour. Jackson Park, located on the South Side of Chicago, Illinois, is where President Barack Obama used to participate in pick-up games. The pair of courts there are situated behind a high chain-link fence, much like The Cages at West Fourth Street in New York City's Greenwich Village, which is also known for its less-than-regulation-size court, encouraging tight defense and long jumpers, with boisterous spectators lining the sidewalk outside.

Venice Beach's famous Blue Court has appeared in movies such as *White Men Can't Jump* and *American History X*. At its location north of the Venice Beach Pier, tall palm trees highlight the scenic vista. Mosswood Park in Oakland, California, helped launch the careers of eleven-time NBA champion Bill Russell and famed point guard Jason Kidd. It is also the yard in which legendary streetballer Demetrius "Hook" Mitchell executed a 360-degree slam dunk over a parked car. The courts at Barry Farms in Washington, DC, spawned the likes of Kevin Durant, while Philadelphia's courts at Sixteenth and Susquehanna Avenue, which could draw five hundred spectators for a tournament game, are the subject of a documentary titled *16th and Philly*.

FILMS

Spike Lee's *He Got Game* (1998) stars Denzel Washington (Jake Shuttlesworth) as the on-screen pops of NBA star Ray Allen (Jesus Shuttlesworth), who was given his name as a tribute to legendary baller Earl "Black Jesus" Monroe. There are several strong scenes revolving around streetball as the father and son work out their substantial problems. *Hoop Dreams* (1994) is an Academy Award–nominated documentary about William Gates and Arthur Agee, a pair of Chicago teens who dream of playing in the NBA. Ultimately, the film uses the backdrop of basketball to explore the issues of class and race in society. It was placed by the *New York Times* on its "Best 1,000 Movies Ever" list. Actors Wesley Snipes (Sidney Deane) and Woody Harrelson (Billy Hoyle) portray street-ball hustlers in the 1992 film *White Men Can't Jump*. Harrelson's Hoyle character helped promote the basketball phrase "in the zone," feeling like you can't miss a shot, among the general public. There is a lot of streetball action, including plenty of comical and in-depth discussion about the mental side of the game. *The Blackout*, a docu-mentary, details the intense rivalry between Fat Joe's Team Terror Squad and Jay Z's Team S. Carter as they vie for the Rucker Park title of 2003, delayed by the largest blackout in the history of North America. Michael Jordan and the Looney Tunes characters join forces in *Space Jam* to defeat the Monstars, an alien squad of ballers that has stolen the skills of some NBA stars, giving the game an interplanetary stage.

MUSIC

Probably the most recognizable piece of music associated with the sport is the new-age theme song "Roundball Rock" from the show *The NBA on NBC* (1990–2002). Despite having no lyrics, the piece, written by composer John Tesh, captured the feel and excitement of the game for audiences worldwide. NBC continues to use the theme song in many other venues, including its coverage of the Olympics. The hip-hop classic "Basketball" by Kurtis Blow is an homage to the sport. The rapper's lyrics take us straight to the heart of the game. "Just like I'm King of the microphone, so is Dr. J and Moses Malone. I like slam dunks, take me to the hoop, my favorite play is the alley-oop." Michael Jackson, aka the King of Pop, used Michael Jordan in the music video of his song "Jam." Even though the piece doesn't feature any real basketball lyrics, the song became associated with the sport through its visuals. The extended version of the video even has a scene with Jackson teaching Jordan to moonwalk. And Ice Cube's classic "It Was a Good Day" ponders the lyrical question "Which park, are y'all playin' basketball?"

BOOKS AND LITERATURE

John Updike penned a masterful poem titled "Ex–Basketball Player." It's about a guy named Flick who is far past his glory days on a high school court and works at a gas station, remembering those magical moments as he dribbles the innertubes of tires. Updike writes, "The ball loved Flick. . . . His hands were like wild birds." *Foul! The Connie Hawkins Story* by David Wolf chronicles the life and times of streetball legend Connie Hawkins. The book follows him from the playgrounds of Brooklyn to his blackballing by the NBA after being wrongly accused in a game-fixing/gambling scandal. It is a riveting and blunt look at basketball and society. *Becoming Kareem: Growing Up on and off the Court* by Kareem Abdul-Jabbar and Raymond Obstfeld details the seven-foot-two basketball superstar's coming of age and dealing with the complex world around him. It is an insightful look at the difficult and challenging journey toward manhood. *Heaven Is a Playground* by Rick Telander shows the poetic and all-consuming side of streetball as a writer arriving to do a magazine piece on a Brooklyn ball yard gets hooked into coaching a team comprised of the local talent. In *You Let Some Girl Beat You?* the iconic and groundbreaking woman player Ann Meyers Drysdale details her triumphs and roadblocks in the game of basketball. The book contains a superb forward by Julius "Dr. J" Erving.

LANGUAGE

Here's a taste of streetball's colorful slang: The basketball is referred to as the "rock" or "pill." Someone who can leap is known to have serious "hops" or "hang time." A player who can dribble the ball well has a "handle," and a good passer is looking to "dish out dimes," assisting his teammates. Scoring the basketball equals "buckets," while someone who shoots without a conscience is a "chucker," often putting up bad shots described as "bricks." A talented player has "skillz." Those waiting on the sideline to play have "next" game. A tarred court is called "the blacktop." The rim and backboard are called "the rack," while the hoop is referred to as the "iron." And a shot that goes in without touching the rim is a "swish," even if there is no netting to make the sound. A high-arching shot is a "rainbow," while a floater with a lesser trajectory is a "teardrop." Tossing the ball to the rim for another player is an "alley-oop." And if it's successful there could be a crowd-rousing "jam" or "slam dunk," which might result in the unlucky defender being "posterized." In the end, though, it's all done to satisfy a competitor's "basketball jones," or intense desire to play.

REFERENCES

Abdul-Jabbar, Kareem. "Kareem Abdul-Jabbar Quotes." BrainyQuote. https://www.brainyquote.com/quotes/kareem_abduljabbar_370688.

Alson, Rafer. "Skip to My Lou." *USA Today*.

Barkley, Charles. "I'm Not a Role Model." Quote Catalog. https://quotecatalog.com/quote/charles-barkley-im-not-a-role-8ab0e87.

Barrington, Raul. "Rafer Alston: 'Streetball Kept the City Alive.'" HoopsHype. July 19, 2013. https://hoopshype.com/2013/07/19/rafer-alston-streetball-kept-the-city-alive/.

Benbow, Dana Hunsinger. "Ann Meyers Took Her Best Shot at Making the Pacers." *IndyStar*. June 4, 2015. https://www.indystar.com/story/sports/nba/pacers/2015/06/02/ann-meyers-took-best-shot-making-pacers/28345597.

Bogues, Tyrone. "Muggsy Bogues Quotes." BrainyQuote. https://www.brainyquote.com/quotes/muggsy_bogues_966707.

"Bred With Toughness in the True Mecca of Basketball." Video uploaded to YouTube by Ballislife on August 20, 2017. https://www.youtube.com/watch?v=4ExPko0_N5o.

"Carol Blazejowski on Following Your Passion." Video posted to YouTube by Official-Hoophall on December 7, 2016. https://www.youtube.com/watch?v=s6dlh0KTGU4.

"Cheryl Miller Speaks on the Lessons of Basketball." Video uploaded to YouTube by *Los Angeles Sentinel Newspaper* on June 10, 2016. https://www.youtube.com/watch?v=weQ8nCvvnSs.

Elmore, Jemal. Episode #41: "Hot Sauce." Blog Talk Radio. February 22, 2011. https://www.blogtalkradio.com/inthezonesportsshow/2011/02/22/hot-sauce-1.

Frazier, Walt "Clyde," and Dan Markowitz. *The Game within the Game*. New York: Hyperion, 2006.

James, LeBron. https://babchem.wordpress.com/life-quotes-1.

Jordan, Michael. "Michael Jordan Quotes." BrainyQuote. https://www.brainyquote.com/quotes/michael_jordan_447194.

———. "Michael Jordan Quotes." BrainyQuote. https://www.brainyquote.com/quotes/michael_jordan_167377.

Lieberman, Nancy. NBATV interview, August 2016.

Lyons, Ben. "The Professor." *The Players Tribune: Real Fan Life*. June 16, 2015. https://www.theplayerstribune.com/en-us/articles/the-professor-grayson-boucher-streetball.

Mallozzi, Vincent. "The Legend of Pee Wee Kirkland Grows." *New York Times*. January 12, 1997. https://www.nytimes.com/1997/01/12/sports/the-legend-of-pee-wee-kirkland-grows.html.

Malone, Karl. "One Role Model to Another." *Sports Illustrated*. June 14, 1993. https://www.si.com/vault/1993/06/14/128740/one-role-model-to-another-whether-he-likes-it-or-not-charles-barkley-sets-an-example-that-many-will-follow.

Meyers Drysdale, Ann, and Joni Ravenna. *You Let Some Girl Beat You? The Story of Ann Meyers Drysdale*. Lake Forest, CA: Belcher Publications 2012.

"Mike   Krzyzewski   Quotes."   Sports   Feel   Good   Stories.   https://www.sportsfeelgoodstories.com/mike-krzyzewski-quotes.

"Nate Robinson Talk 'Heart over Height.'" Video posted to YouTube by ThePostGame on June 18, 2014. https://www.youtube.com/watch?v=Ff__4sU8eHA.

NBA.com Staff. "Legends Profile: Nate Archibald." NBA.com. https://www.nba.com/history/legends/profiles/nate-archibald.

"New York Streetball: Played Real Hard." Video uploaded to YouTube by bepfen1 on May 31, 2013. https://www.youtube.com/watch?v=opGiIryUsIc.

Nuckols, Ben. "Coach Kobe: Bryant Shares Philosophies on How to Reach Kids." *Business Insider*. October 16, 2018, https://www.businessinsider.com/ap-coach-kobe-bryant-shares-philosophies-on-how-to-reach-kids-2018-10.

"Pee Wee Kirkland on Being a Basketball Star While Running a Drug Empire." Video uploaded to YouTube by djvlad on March 14, 2016. https://www.youtube.com/watch?v=YLRIdAL0Je8.

"Rafer Alston (Skip to My Lou) Streetball Legends." Video posted to YouTube by Face PC   Gaming.   September   22,   2017.   https://www.youtube.com/watch?v=BripuBjLbQM.

"Shammgod (Crossover to God) Full Video Interview | Streets First." Video uploaded to YouTube by Streets First Podcast on January 17, 2018. https://www.youtube.com/watch?v=euv7wmPsbBM.

"Sheryl Swoopes—60 Days of Summer 2015." Video uploaded to YouTube by Official-Hoophall on August 13, 2015. https://www.youtube.com/watch?v=M1NCIo7IlYE.

Shultz, Alex. "Streetball Legend The Professor Still Making Moves." *Bleacher Report*. January 26, 2018. https://bleacherreport.com/articles/2755958-streetball-legend-the-professor-still-making-moves.

"60 Days of Summer—Julius Erving." Video posted to YouTube by OfficialHoophall on September 2, 2016. https://www.youtube.com/watch?v=VNuWpn730Go.

Smallwood, Karl. "The Greatest Basketball Player You've Probably Never Heard Of." TodayIFoundOut.com. June 18, 2015. http://www.todayifoundout.com/index.php/2015/06/earl-manigault-greatest-basketball-player-youve-never-heard.

ABOUT THE AUTHOR

Paul Volponi is a writer, educator, and journalist living in New York City. He is the author of twelve novels for young adults and the recipient of twelve American Library Association Honors. *Black and White* is the winner of the International Reading Association's Children's Book Award. That novel of social justice was inspired by the six years the author worked on Rikers Island, teaching incarcerated teens to read and write. *The Final Four*, about the NCAA Men's Basketball Tournament, received five starred reviews and is on the New York City Chancellor's Ninth-Grade Reading List (NYC Reads 365). *Top Prospect*, a middle-grade novel about an eighth grader given an early college football scholarship, is part of Scholastic's nationwide book club. The author's first nonfiction book, *That's My Team! The History, Science, and Fun behind Sports Teams' Names* (also published by Rowman & Littlefield) was the subject of an extended article in the August 2019 edition of *VOYA*, the nation's premier journal for librarians.

Volponi holds an MA in American literature from the City College of New York and a BA in English from Baruch. You can read excerpts from all his YA works, discover their origins, and read the author's notes at http://paulvolponibooks.com or visit him on Facebook.